OPPOSING VIEWPOINTS® SERIES

Islamic Militancy

Other Books of Related Interest:

Opposing Viewpoints Series
Human Rights

Terrorism

At Issue Series
Does the World Hate the U.S.?

National Security

Should Governments Negotiate with Terrorists?

Current Controversies Series
Homeland Security

Middle East

Global Viewpoints Series
The War in Iraq

Introducing Issues with Opposing Viewpoints Series
Hate Crimes

Islam

Middle East

The Patriot Act

Terrorism

"Congress shall make
no law. . .abridging the
freedom of speech, or
of the press."

First Amendment to the U.S. Constitution

The basic foundation of our democracy is the First Amendment guarantee of freedom of expression. The *Opposing Viewpoints* Series is dedicated to the concept of this basic freedom and the idea that it is more important to practice it than to enshrine it.

OPPOSING
VIEWPOINTS®
SERIES

| Islamic Militancy

Amanda Hiber, Book Editor

GREENHAVEN PRESS
A part of Gale, Cengage Learning

GALE
CENGAGE Learning™

Detroit • New York • San Francisco • New Haven, Conn • Waterville, Maine • London

Christine Nasso, *Publisher*
Elizabeth Des Chenes, *Managing Editor*

© 2009 Greenhaven Press, a part of Gale, Cengage Learning

Gale and Greenhaven Press are registered trademarks used herein under license.

For more information, contact:
Greenhaven Press
27500 Drake Rd.
Farmington Hills, MI 48331-3535
Or you can visit our Internet site at gale.cengage.com

For product information and technology assistance, contact us at

Gale Customer Support, 1-800-877-4253
For permission to use material from this text or product, submit all requests online at www.cengage.com/permissions

Further permissions questions can be emailed to permissionrequest@cengage.com

Articles in Greenhaven Press anthologies are often edited for length to meet page requirements. In addition, original titles of these works are changed to clearly present the main thesis and to explicitly indicate the author's opinion. Every effort is made to ensure that Greenhaven Press accurately reflects the original intent of the authors. Every effort has been made to trace the owners of copyrighted material.

Cover image © Warrick Page/Corbis.

LIBRARY OF CONGRESS CATALOGING-IN-PUBLICATION DATA

Islamic militancy / Amanda Hiber, book editor.
    p. cm. -- (Opposing viewpoints)
    Includes bibliographical references and index.
    ISBN 978-0-7377-4216-9 (hbk.)
    ISBN 978-0-7377-4217-6 (pbk.)
    1. Terrorism--Islamic countries--Juvenile literature. 2. Terrorism--Religious aspects--Islam--Juvenile literature. 3. Islamic fundamentalism--Juvenile literature. I. Hiber, Amanda.
    HV6433.I74185 2009
    363.325088'297--dc22
                                                      2009003281

Printed in the United States of America
1 2 3 4 5 6 7 13 12 11 10 09

Contents

Chapter 2: Does the Qur'an Encourage Islamic Militancy?

Chapter 3: How Should Western Governments Respond to Islamic Militancy?

Chapter 4: How Should Citizens Respond to Islamic Militancy?

Why Consider Opposing Viewpoints?

> *"The only way in which a human being can make some approach to knowing the whole of a subject is by hearing what can be said about it by persons of every variety of opinion and studying all modes in which it can be looked at by every character of mind. No wise man ever acquired his wisdom in any mode but this."*
>
> *John Stuart Mill*

In our media-intensive culture it is not difficult to find differing opinions. Thousands of newspapers and magazines and dozens of radio and television talk shows resound with differing points of view. The difficulty lies in deciding which opinion to agree with and which "experts" seem the most credible. The more inundated we become with differing opinions and claims, the more essential it is to hone critical reading and thinking skills to evaluate these ideas. Opposing Viewpoints books address this problem directly by presenting stimulating debates that can be used to enhance and teach these skills. The varied opinions contained in each book examine many different aspects of a single issue. While examining these conveniently edited opposing views, readers can develop critical thinking skills such as the ability to compare and contrast authors' credibility, facts, argumentation styles, use of persuasive techniques, and other stylistic tools. In short, the Opposing Viewpoints Series is an ideal way to attain the higher-level thinking and reading skills so essential in a culture of diverse and contradictory opinions.

In addition to providing a tool for critical thinking, Opposing Viewpoints books challenge readers to question their own strongly held opinions and assumptions. Most people form their opinions on the basis of upbringing, peer pressure, and personal, cultural, or professional bias. By reading carefully balanced opposing views, readers must directly confront new ideas as well as the opinions of those with whom they disagree. This is not to simplistically argue that everyone who reads opposing views will—or should—change his or her opinion. Instead, the series enhances readers' understanding of their own views by encouraging confrontation with opposing ideas. Careful examination of others' views can lead to the readers' understanding of the logical inconsistencies in their own opinions, perspective on why they hold an opinion, and the consideration of the possibility that their opinion requires further evaluation.

Evaluating Other Opinions

To ensure that this type of examination occurs, Opposing Viewpoints books present all types of opinions. Prominent spokespeople on different sides of each issue as well as well-known professionals from many disciplines challenge the reader. An additional goal of the series is to provide a forum for other, less known, or even unpopular viewpoints. The opinion of an ordinary person who has had to make the decision to cut off life support from a terminally ill relative, for example, may be just as valuable and provide just as much insight as a medical ethicist's professional opinion. The editors have two additional purposes in including these less known views. One, the editors encourage readers to respect others' opinions—even when not enhanced by professional credibility. It is only by reading or listening to and objectively evaluating others' ideas that one can determine whether they are worthy of consideration. Two, the inclusion of such viewpoints encourages the important critical thinking skill of objectively evaluating an author's credentials and bias. This evaluation will illuminate an author's reasons for taking a particular stance on an issue and will aid in readers' evaluation of the author's ideas.

It is our hope that these books will give readers a deeper understanding of the issues debated and an appreciation of the complexity of even seemingly simple issues when good and honest people disagree. This awareness is particularly important in a democratic society such as ours in which people enter into public debate to determine the common good. Those with whom one disagrees should not be regarded as enemies but rather as people whose views deserve careful examination and may shed light on one's own.

Thomas Jefferson once said that "difference of opinion leads to inquiry, and inquiry to truth." Jefferson, a broadly educated man, argued that "if a nation expects to be ignorant and free . . . it expects what never was and never will be." As individuals and as a nation, it is imperative that we consider the opinions of others and examine them with skill and discernment. The Opposing Viewpoints Series is intended to help readers achieve this goal.

David L. Bender and Bruno Leone,
Founders

Introduction

> *"Terrorism is as old as the story of mankind."*
>
> —*Walter Laqueur,*
> *"World of Terror,"*
> National Geographic, *Nov. 2004*

When Islamic terrorists hijacked four commercial airplanes and crashed two of them into the twin towers of the World Trade Center in midtown Manhattan and one airplane into the Pentagon in Washington, D.C., Americans—along with the rest of the world—were shocked. But to many Americans, the shock did not simply come from the lack of warning or the scale of the attacks. To many, the intent behind the attack was the greatest surprise. As reporter Laura Miller wrote in her September 27, 2001, *Salon* article: "Adding to the shock of thousands of violent deaths was the bewildering information that the people who so passionately want us dead belong to nations and groups that many Americans had never even heard of." Indeed, in the weeks following the attacks, several news outlets reported violent acts of vengeance carried out by Americans against Sikhs they mistook for Muslims because of their beards and turbans. In the September 29, 2001, *New York Daily News*, Maki Becker reported, "Already, more than 200 bias incidents against Sikhs have been reported nationwide." Indeed, in the British newspaper *The Independent*, Andrew Gumbel wrote in October of that same year of "Americans' ignorance of the sheer anger and resentment that their government's policies have stirred up around the world."

The perception of many in America that Islamic militants had only just come out of the woodwork, in fact, belies reality. A U.S. State Department document, "Significant Terrorist Incidents, 1961–2003: A Brief Chronology," listed at least ten terrorist attacks by Islamic militant groups in Western nations alone. Such attacks include the Munich Olympics massacre in 1972, the hijacking of a TWA flight from Rome to Athens in 1985, and the World Trade Center Bombing in 1993. Americans also were targeted by Islamic militants in the Iran hostage crisis of 1979, the bombings of the U.S. Embassy in Beirut in 1983, and attacks on two U.S. embassies in East Africa in 1998, and the attack on the U.S.S. *Cole* in 2000. A 2006 report by the U.S. Counterterrorism Center concluded that of all the fatalities due to terrorist attacks in 2005, 25 percent could be attributed to Islamic extremist groups.

The roots of Islamic militancy are highly debated and, most likely, varied. Many people believe that it is simply a reaction to Western governments' self-serving and intrusive foreign policy in the Middle East, including the United States's support of Israel. In his 2006 article "We Must Acknowledge the Roots of Terror," Ramzy Baroud explained, "What is radicalization but a culmination of bitterness, resentment and anger that lurk desperately inside, which often translate to despicable behavior: terrorism?" Others believe that the Muslim holy book, the Qur'an, actually calls for terrorism in the name of God. Still others cite Muslims' history of imperialism, or anti-Semitism, as the source of Islamic militancy. Although there probably never will be a consensus reached about the causes of Islamic militancy, there is no doubt that discussion about the factors that contribute to it has grown since the September 11, 2001, attacks.

In post-9/11 America, Islamic militant attacks that may have previously fallen below the radar now no longer do. There has not been another terrorist attack on American soil since September 11, but other Western nations have not been spared. On March 11, 2004, 191 people were killed and 1,841 were wounded when bombs exploded on four commuter trains in Madrid, Spain. Spanish officials believe a group linked to al-Qaeda was responsible for the attacks. On July 7, 2005, four British-born Muslim terrorists bombed underground trains and a double-decker bus in London, England, killing 52 and injuring at least 770 people. Only one year later, on August 10, 2006, London police thwarted another terrorist attack aimed at as many as ten aircraft scheduled to fly between Britain and the United States.

For much of America, the world became a larger and scarier place on September 11, 2001. In fact, a poll conducted by CBS News and *The New York Times* in 2006 found that 39 percent of Americans polled said they feel less safe than they did in 2001. If Americans are to face their fears in the world outside the United States, they must become more informed, less sheltered global citizens. To this end, it is imperative that they learn about ideologies and values of various peoples across the globe, including those behind Islamic militancy. In the chapters that follow, the questions, What Factors Contribute to Islamic Militancy? Does the Qur'an Encourage Islamic Militancy? How Should Western Governments Respond to Islamic Militancy? and How Should Citizens Respond to Islamic Militancy? are explored and debated. The viewpoints responding to these questions present valuable information and unique perspectives on the crucial and timely topic of Islamic militancy.

CHAPTER 1

What Factors Contribute to Islamic Militancy?

Chapter Preface

American politicians, pundits, and citizens have vigorously debated the sources of Islamic militancy even before the morning of September 11, 2001. Terrorist acts by fundamentalist Muslims have been blamed on Islamic scripture, poverty, foreign policy, lack of education, and cultural clashes. Yet any search for the source of Islamic militancy seems incomplete without putting the question to the militants themselves. To what, in fact, do Islamic militants attribute their acts of terrorism?

In his November 2002 "Letter to the American People," published in *The Observer*, Osama bin Laden, the mastermind of the September 11, 2001, attacks, answers this question directly: "Because you attacked us and continue to attack us." Indeed, the dominant theme in Osama bin Laden's messages is that the attacks are acts of retribution for American (and other Western countries') foreign policy decisions. A BBC transcript of an April 2004 audiotape reports bin Laden saying: "Our acts are reaction to your own acts, which are represented by the destruction and killing of our kinfolk in Afghanistan, Iraq and Palestine." Abu Musab al-Zarqawi, a leader of al-Qaeda in Iraq, repeats this message in a 2006 video: "You will never live in peace until we live in peace," he says, according to a CNN transcript.

Beyond recent foreign policy, Islamic militants also refer to centuries of Western imperialism as precipitating the outrage that has led to terrorism. In a November 2001 video, bin Laden says, "Following World War I, which ended more than 83 years ago, the whole Islamic world fell under the crusader banner—under the British, French, and Italian governments. They divided the whole world, and Palestine was occupied by the British. Since then, and for more than 83 years, our brothers, sons, and sisters in Palestine have been badly tortured."

Indeed, the Israel-Palestine war is the primary foreign policy grievance cited by Islamic militants.

Less frequently mentioned in the proselytizations of Islamic militants are reactions to Western lifestyles and value systems. Bin Laden's 2002 letter calls on Americans "to stop your oppression, lies, immorality and debauchery that has spread among you...We call you to be a people of manners, principles, honour, and purity; to reject the immoral acts of fornication, homosexuality, intoxicants, gambling's [sic], and trading with interest."

While the weight these statements should be given is surely arguable, it is worth noting that the justifications made by Islamic militants echo the analyses of many of the commentators in this chapter. Whether or not these explanations justify the actions of Islamic militants is, of course, another debate entirely.

"The United States played a major role in unleashing the global Islamic jihad now focused on our country."

U.S. Foreign Policy Has Contributed to the Rise of Islamic Militancy

Dimitri K. Simes

In this viewpoint, Nixon Center founder and National Interest *publisher Dimitri K. Simes asserts that the foreign policies of current and recent U.S. presidents have contributed significantly to the terrorist threat America now faces. After a CIA operation authorized by President Carter provoked the Soviet invasion of Afghanistan, he argues, the U.S. government went on to support the Afghan mujahideen resistance movement, of which al-Qaeda is an outgrowth. According to the author, subsequent administrations failed to correct these mistakes and continued supporting groups that would later pose a great threat to the American people.*

As you read, consider the following questions:

1. To whom did the Reagan administration outsource its support for the mujahideen in Afghanistan?

Dimitri K. Simes, "Jihad, Unintended," *National Interest Online*, Winter 2005/2006. www.nationalinterest.org. Copyright © 2006 *National Interest*. Reproduced with permission.

2. According to Simes, what were the unintended results of the Kosovo War of 1999?

3. Why does Zbigniew Brzezinski oppose U.S. cooperation with Russia against radical Islam, in Simes's opinion?

How President [George W.] Bush and his team handle the three remaining years [2006–8] of his tenure in office—especially their efforts to deal with the interrelated problems of terrorism, proliferation and the war in Iraq—will have a major impact not only on his legacy but, more importantly, on American security. Whether a distracted White House can undertake a hard-headed assessment of these problems, give them the priority they deserve, and find ways to work more effectively with others, especially other major powers, remains to be seen.

Regrettably, this administration and recent administrations of both parties have fallen far short in dealing with the danger of extremist terror. In fact, as most Americans would be shocked to learn, the United States played a major role in unleashing the global Islamic jihad now focused on our country. Surely no American policymaker ever sought a radical Islamist assault on the United States—yet several successive administrations undertook multiple policy sins of both commission and omission that helped the jihad to become established, to gain momentum, and finally to flourish virtually unopposed until it hit New York and Washington.

Still, instead of learning from past mistakes, we seem hellbent on celebrating them. Some of the current administration's most vocal critics conveniently disregard their own responsibility for the emergence of the anti-American jihad. Worse, they press for policies that increase American vulnerabilities at a time when terrorists are trying to acquire nuclear weapons.

Many realize that Al-Qaeda grew in part from the mujaheddin Washington armed and supported to drive out the Soviet Union after its 1979 invasion of Afghanistan. But few are aware of the full impact of U.S. decisions at key points both before and after the Soviet intervention—decisions taken by several successive U.S. administrations—that unintentionally breathed life into this Frankenstein monster.

U.S. Provoked, Then Fought, the Invasion

According to former National Security Advisor Zbigniew Brzezinski, now one of the most acerbic critics of President Bush's handling of both Iraq and radical Islam, the [Jimmy] Carter Administration authorized a covert CIA [Central Intelligence Agency] operation, notwithstanding an expectation that it would provoke a Soviet invasion of Afghanistan. In an interview in *Le Nouvel Observateur* in 1998, Brzezinski said that clandestine U.S. involvement in Afghanistan began months before the Soviet invasion; in fact, he added, he wrote a note to President Carter predicting that "this aid was going to induce a Soviet military intervention." As Brzezinski put it, "we didn't push the Russians to intervene, but we knowingly increased the probability that they would." And even in hindsight, Brzezinski thought "that secret operation was an excellent idea", because "it had the effect of drawing the Russians into the Afghan trap" and exploited "the opportunity of giving the USSR its Vietnam War" [unpopular war involving the United States from 1959 to 1975 in which the U.S. failed to achieve its goal].

Of course, this is not what the Carter Administration told Congress or the American people at the time.

In view of Soviet expansionism elsewhere, the United States had little choice but to fight the invasion of Afghanistan once it occurred. But supporting resistance to a Soviet occupation is very different from intentionally "increasing the probability" of a Soviet invasion.

More recently, Brzezinski has acknowledged that one of his motives in entangling the Soviet Union in Afghanistan was promoting the liberation of Central Europe by diverting Soviet attention from responding more forcefully to Solidarity's [Polish trade union/political movement] challenge. Yet, desirable as this end might have been, one may question whether it justified using means that would provoke an almost decade-long war in Afghanistan that both devastated the country and jump-started a global Islamic jihad against America.

Reagan Continued Policy Errors

Nevertheless, the Carter Administration was not alone in making mistakes in Afghanistan. The [Ronald] Reagan Administration's decision to "outsource" responsibility for arming and organizing the resistance to Pakistan's intelligence service and Saudi-funded foreign mujaheddin was insufficiently thought out. Though no one could reasonably have been expected to predict that the same groups would attack New York twenty-some years later, stronger reservations were appropriate in the wake of the Iranian revolution, which showed very clearly how easily Muslim extremists could turn against the United States. It was also no secret that some of the mujaheddin commanders in Afghanistan were, even during the 1980s, already talking about establishing an Islamic caliphate and about the United States being next on the receiving end of their righteous zeal.

This lack of sober evaluation explains why, when the United States had an opportunity to try to put the Islamist genie back into the bottle, we failed to take it. In 1988 [Soviet head of state] Mikhail Gorbachev decided to withdraw Soviet troops from Afghanistan and was looking for a face-saving solution that would create a coalition government in Kabul to avoid chaos and prevent Pakistani-supported Muslim extremists from taking over the country. The feasibility of a coalition government is substantiated by the fact that even after the withdrawal of Soviet troops, the [Mohammad] Najibullah regime managed to control Kabul for over three years. With a modicum of U.S. support, a coalition government in Afghanistan could have been created that would probably have prevented the Taliban's rise to power, with consequences for Al-Qaeda's ability to operate in Afghanistan with impunity.

Decisions Driven by Politics

Yet despite the efforts of Jack Matlock, then-U.S. ambassador to the USSR [Union of Soviet Socialist Republics], the Reagan Administration rejected the Soviet attempt to find a negotiated solution to the Afghan war by insisting that for the United States to end its support of the mujaheddin, Moscow had not only to withdraw its troops but to cut off military assistance to the Afghan government. As Matlock writes in his book *Reagan and Gorbachev: How the Cold War Ended* (2005), "The U.S. attitude [toward Afghanistan] was driven more by politics in Washington than by the situation in Afghanistan", since it was clear that if Soviet troops could not defeat the Afghan resistance, the Soviet-backed regime "could hardly do so whether or not it received additional military supplies from Moscow." Indeed, as Matlock continues:

> The main issue for the Americans had always been the Soviet military occupation. If that ended, there was no good reason for the United States to continue giving arms to some Afghan factions whose aims, other than expelling Soviet military forces from their country, were remote from any American interests.

But this viewpoint was rejected. Brzezinski, for example, was quite critical of President Reagan's alleged willingness to "play along" with the Soviet "game" of using arms control concessions to improve Moscow's image while threatening "the stability of Pakistan" and seeking "dominance over the Persian Gulf region"—this at a time when perestroika [a period of economic reforms in the Soviet Union] was already well underway and it was clear that Soviet "new thinking" in foreign policy was demonstrably for real.

Today's Insurgents in Iraq Are Tomorrow's Terrorists

When the United States started sending guns and money to the Afghan mujahideen in the 1980s, it had a clearly defined Cold War purpose: helping expel the Soviet army, which had invaded Afghanistan in 1979. And so it made sense that once the Afghan jihad forced a Soviet withdrawal a decade later, Washington would lose interest in the rebels. For the international mujahideen drawn to the Afghan conflict, however, the fight was just beginning. They opened new fronts in the name of global jihad and became the spearhead of Islamist terrorism. The seriousness of the blowback became clear to the United States with the 1993 bombing of the World Trade Center: all of the attack's participants either had served in Afghanistan or were linked to a Brooklyn-based fund-raising organ for the Afghan jihad that was later revealed to be al Qaeda's de facto U.S. headquarters. The blowback, evident in other countries as well, continued to increase in intensity throughout the rest of the decade, culminating on September 11, 2001.

The current war in Iraq will generate a ferocious blowback of its own, which—as a recent classified CIA assessment predicts—could be longer and more powerful than that from Afghanistan.

Peter Bergen and Alec Reynolds, "Blowback Revisited," Foreign Affairs, Nov.–Dec. 2005.

Second Chance Squandered

Though history rarely gives second chances, the United States did have another opportunity to blunt Islamic extremism in

25

Afghanistan in the 1990s. While few still take seriously [professor of international political economy] Francis Fukuyama's claim that history ended with the U.S.-led Western victory in the Cold War, there is no doubt that the absence of the apocalyptic Soviet challenge gave America considerably greater freedom of choice in defining its foreign policy priorities.

One would have thought that the World Trade Center bombing in 1993, the simultaneous attacks on U.S. embassies in Africa in 1998 and the strike on the USS *Cole* in 2000, among other incidents, would have alerted policymakers that a new major challenge to American interests and American lives was in the making. However, instead of combating this threat, the United States focused on "wars of choice" and haphazard attempts to "nation-build" in the Balkans.

The architects of this tragic diversion are unrepentant and even proud of what they have done. As Richard Holbrooke, the person largely responsible for shaping a flawed U.S. policy in the Balkans, wrote in the *Washington Post* in July 2005, "Was Bosnia worth it? As we approach the 10th anniversary of Dayton [the Bosnia-Herzegovina Peace Agreement was reached outside of Dayton, Ohio in November 1995], there should no longer be any debate."

Holbrooke's claim that there should be no debate about Bosnia demonstrates his chutzpah, but it does not pass even minimal analytic scrutiny. If the United States had wanted to stop the war, it could have supported the Vance-Owen plan [which would have divided Bosnia into ten semi-autonomous regions]—rejected by the Clinton Administration at the time as allegedly too favorable to the Serbs. And given the administration's inaction on genocide in Rwanda, it is not surprising that major powers like China and Russia found it difficult to accept that humanitarian considerations alone motivated the United States to act, first in Bosnia, then in Kosovo, especially when American protégés engaged in ethnic cleansing operations of their own.

Misplaced Priorities

The "unintended consequences" of the Kosovo war in 1999 were to poison U.S. relations with Russia and China alike, leading eventually to the Clinton Administration's contemptuous rejection of Russian proposals for joint action against the Taliban and Al-Qaeda—proposals that resurfaced after 9/11 [terrorist attacks of September 11, 2001] and eventually contributed to removing the Taliban from power.

In the aftermath of 9/11, the Bush Administration appropriately, if belatedly, broke with the past by identifying the fight against radical Islamic terrorism as America's top foreign policy priority—and by understanding that at times hard choices have to be made to secure America. Yet that commitment has weakened, in part under a steady barrage of domestic criticism from senior members of the American foreign policy community.

Mr. Brzezinski remains preoccupied with the danger of U.S.-Russian cooperation against radical Islam because it might give Moscow undeserved legitimacy, especially in dealing with Chechnya, and prevent the United States from further containment of Russia within its own geographic neighborhood. Yet without working together with the [Vladimir] Putin government, how can the United States hope to safeguard Russian stockpiles of nuclear materials, continue to work with Moscow to secure Soviet nuclear materials in other countries, or persuade Russia to sacrifice its economic stake in nuclear cooperation with Iran?

Potential Consequences

Mr. Holbrooke wants the United States to support independence for Kosovo, whether the democratic Serbian government accepts it or not. But what if ignoring Serbian objections discredits the moderate and pro-Western politicians now leading the country and results in a rabidly nationalist government there, reopening the Balkan can of worms? What if

Russia takes the predictable position that what is good for Kosovo should be good for other unrecognized but de facto independent [former Soviet] states such as Nagorno-Karabakh or the Transdniester Republic? What of separatist regions like South Ossetia and Abkhazia, which share borders with Russia and where local populations overwhelmingly do not want to be a part of Georgia? In the latter case, the United States would face a series of unpleasant choices. Would the United States, in the name of principle, compel a pro-American Georgian regime to abandon its desire to restore the country's territorial integrity? Or would Washington side with Tbilisi [the Capital of the Republic of Georgia], especially if it decides to use force to recapture these regions? If the latter, the United States could find itself embroiled in a major dispute with Russia that could effectively end cooperation on other matters of vital importance to the United States. And how would the United States force a resolution granting independence to Kosovo through the UN [United Nations] Security Council over probable Chinese objections, without offering guarantees that Taiwan will never become a separate, independent state? Or argue that Kosovo deserves full independence without setting a dangerous precedent that the Kurds of Iraq and Turkey may seek to emulate? The potential for trouble seems serious and real.

The Sorcerer's Apprentice

As the world's only superpower, the United States can have a profound influence—deliberately and inadvertently—on the international system and many of its component parts. Yet America is not unlike the Sorcerer's Apprentice in its ability to set in motion forces so momentous that it may lack the power to stop or divert them. Because there is no sorcerer to rescue us from the unintended results of our actions, we have a special responsibility to consider our policies very carefully.

In the case of the War on Terror, we have already made several key errors and cannot turn back the clock. It is a reality that terrorists who openly view the United States as their enemy are working very hard to arm themselves with nuclear weapons. But we can still take this problem much more seriously than we have, by making it an organizing principle of U.S. foreign policy. Policies that unacceptably increase the risk of attacks, or weaken our already incomplete efforts at non-proliferation for secondary gains, should be reassessed.

President Bush recently equated Islamic radicalism with "Islamofascism" and drew parallels between the War on Terror and World War II. If senior administration officials truly believe those comparisons, they should establish American priorities accordingly. [President] Franklin Delano Roosevelt and [British Prime Minister] Winston Churchill were both idealists deeply committed to democracy and Western values, but they also understood the importance of defeating the Nazi menace—and this realization shaped their other policy decisions. In protecting U.S. national security, idealistic claims are not a substitute for realistic and honest analysis, nor for courage on the part of policymakers to act upon it, domestic pressures notwithstanding.

> *"Policymakers must recognize that intervention—particularly the prolonged intervention being planned for Iraq— vastly expands the pool of people willing to listen to, and follow, terrorist demagogues."*

The Iraq War Has Contributed to the Rise in Islamic Militancy

Doug Bandow

In this viewpoint, Doug Bandow argues that the Iraq war has not only failed to reduce the terrorist threat; it has contributed to its increase by attracting more recruits to the terrorists' cause. He argues that although some attacks may have other triggers, the vast majority of them are in response to U.S. foreign policy in nations like Iraq. Bandow is a former senior fellow at the Cato Institute and a frequent political commentator for CNN, MSNBC, Fortune *magazine, and other media outlets.*

As you read, consider the following questions:

1. How does Bandow assess the George W. Bush administration's response to 9/11?

2. According to Robert Pape's book, cited by Bandow, what is the most common goal of terrorist attacks?

3. Besides providing a recruitment tool, how else is the Iraq war helping extremist groups, according to Bandow?

President George W. Bush has launched a campaign to shore up flagging support for the occupation of Iraq. "Our troops," he intoned in his weekly radio address Saturday [August 20, 2005], are fighting "to protect their fellow Americans from a savage enemy." Indeed, he added, "if we do not confront these evil men abroad, we will have to face them one day in our own cities and streets." This continues a theme he laid out in Fort Bragg recently [June 28, 2005]: "We fight today because terrorists want to attack our country and kill our citizens, and Iraq is where they are making their stand."

Unfortunately, the dual attacks in London . . . [on July 7, 2005] clearly showed that the Iraq war has not reduced the terrorist threat.

Too many Americans and Iraqis already have died based on false claims about [Iraqi president] Saddam Hussein's supposed possession of WMDs [weapons of mass destruction] and connection to 9/11 [September 11, 2001, terrorist attacks on the United States]. No one should die now under the illusion that we are fighting terrorists in Baghdad and Fallujah instead of New York and London.

A Terrorist Recruitment Tool

Terrorists who kill and maim should themselves be killed or captured—whether they are operating in London, Baghdad, or New York. Which is why the administration's initial response to 9/11—targeting al-Qaeda and overthrowing the Taliban in Afghanistan—was entirely appropriate.

But battling terrorism should not mean fighting blind or basing policy on delusions. In general, terrorism is a violent tool in a political struggle, where one side is overmatched in conventional terms. Robert Pape, author of the new book, *Dying to Win*, reviewed 315 suicide bombing attacks between 1983 and 2003 and found that virtually all of them had "a specific secular and strategic goal: to compel democracies to withdraw military forces from the terrorists' national homeland."

There are undoubtedly jihadists who simply hate America and its freedoms. A few others might have wild ideas about reestablishing Islamic glory over Western lands. But the evidence suggests that most of the antagonism springs from hatred of U.S. (and allied) government policies.

For instance, before the London bombings a British intelligence assessment leaked to the press found that "events in Iraq are continuing to act as motivation and a focus of a range of terrorist-related activity." In a new report Britain's Chatham House observes that Iraq has given "a boost to the al-Qaeda network's propaganda, recruitment and fundraising."

The Israeli Global Research in International Affairs Center reported earlier this year [2005] that Iraq "has turned into a magnet for jihadi volunteers." But not established terrorists. Rather, explained report author Reuven Paz, "the vast majority of Arabs killed in Iraq have never taken part in any terrorist activity prior to their arrival in Iraq."

Larry Johnson, who served with both the CIA [Central Intelligence Agency] and the State Department's counterterrorism office, observes, "You now in Iraq have a recruiting ground in which jihadists, people who previously were not willing to go out and embrace the vision of bin Laden" are "now aligning themselves with elements that have declared allegiance to him."

The British government recently compiled an extensive report entitled "Young Muslims and Extremism," warning that British-U.S. policies are alienating many Muslims who see

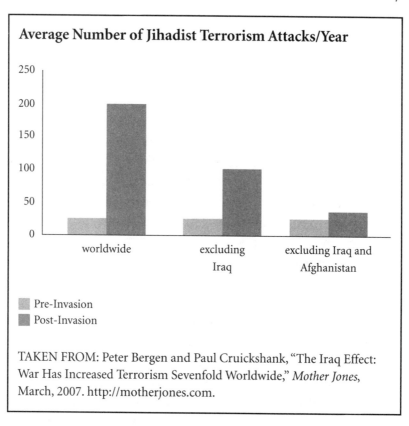

Average Number of Jihadist Terrorism Attacks/Year

Pre-Invasion
Post-Invasion

TAKEN FROM: Peter Bergen and Paul Cruickshank, "The Iraq Effect: War Has Increased Terrorism Sevenfold Worldwide," *Mother Jones*, March, 2007. http://motherjones.com.

them "as having been acts against Islam." Analysts informed the prime minister that the Iraq war is acting as a "recruiting sergeant" for extremism.

Providing an Opportunity for More Violence

"The battle experience that jihadists gain in Iraq," Paz adds, "supplies the Islamist adherents of the Global Jihad culture with a wealth of first-hand field experience." Larry Johnson worries that Iraqi insurgents are learning how to build bombs and run military operations.

Even more menacingly, after being trained in the ways of urban warfare, these terrorists are "bleeding out" around the world. Germany's *Der Spiegel* magazine reports that scores of

Muslim extremists have returned to Europe from Iraq, and all "are equipped with fresh combat experience and filled with ideological indoctrination. It is these men who are considered particularly dangerous."

The ideology these men absorb is heavily colored by U.S. and British policies. Al-Qaeda's number two, Ayman Zawahiri, recently denounced "aggression against Muslims," ranging from war to support for corrupt regimes. Osama bin Laden's earlier phrasing was: "If you bomb our cities, we will bomb yours." Although condemning the London attacks, Hamas leader Mahmoud al-Zahar contended that Muslims have suffered "too much from the American aggression."

The point is not that their assessments are accurate or U.S. policies are unjustified. Nor should London and Washington precipitously retreat from Iraq and allow terrorist acts to determine national policy. But policymakers must recognize that intervention—particularly the prolonged intervention being planned for Iraq—vastly expands the pool of people willing to listen to, and follow, terrorist demagogues.

Observes Robert Pape: "Since suicide terrorism is mainly a response to foreign occupation and not Islamic fundamentalism, the use of heavy military force to transform Muslim societies over there, if you would, is only likely to increase the number of suicide terrorists coming at us. . . . Suicide terrorism is not a supply-limited phenomenon where there are just a few hundred around the world willing to do it because they are religious fanatics. It is a demand-driven phenomenon."

The Iraq conflict has become a killing field. But not as war supporters expected. It is providing an opportunity for extremists to kill U.S. troops while learning skills that may eventually be employed in Western lands. Whatever the Iraq conflict is accomplishing, it is not making us safer from terrorism. Either President Bush should stop claiming this or we should stop listening to him.

> *"It's not our tolerance for multicultural-ism that fuels terrorism; it's our toler-ance for the barbarism committed in our name."*

Western Societies' Marginalization of Muslim Immigrants Has Encouraged Islamic Militancy

Naomi Klein

Naomi Klein is a nationally syndicated political columnist and author of two bestsellers, most recently, The Shock Doctrine: The Rise of Disaster Capitalism. *In this viewpoint, she writes that, contrary to the common claim that the July 2005 bombings in Britain were caused by that country's oversensitivity to its ethnic minorities, they were in fact a response to outright rac-ism. Egyptian writer Sayyid Qutb's radical ideology, a major in-tellectual influence on al-Qaeda, was shaped by his experiences of racism in the West. Klein argues that the intolerance and marginalization of ethnic minorities in Western societies breeds terrorism.*

Naomi Klein, "Terror's Greatest Recruitment Tool," *The Nation*, August 29, 2005. www.thenation.com. Reproduced by permission of the author.

As you read, consider the following questions:

1. What did Sayyid Qutb witness in America that left him so bitter?

2. What two main causes of terror, in Klein's opinion, are now being sold as its cure by British Prime Minister Tony Blair?

3. Why are one in five ethnic minorities leaving Britain, according to a *Guardian* poll?

Hussain Osman, one of the men alleged to have participated in London's failed bombings on July 21, [2005] recently told Italian investigators that they prepared for the attacks by watching "films on the war in Iraq," *La Repubblica* reported. "Especially those where women and children were being killed and exterminated by British and American soldiers. . .of widows, mothers and daughters that cry."

It has become an article of faith that Britain was vulnerable to terror because of its politically correct antiracism. Yet Osman's comments suggest that what propelled at least some of the bombers was rage at what they saw as extreme racism. And what else can we call the belief—so prevalent we barely notice it—that American and European lives are worth more than the lives of Arabs and Muslims, so much more that their deaths in Iraq are not even counted?

It's not the first time that this kind of raw inequality has bred extremism. Sayyid Qutb, the Egyptian writer generally viewed as the intellectual architect of radical political Islam, had his ideological epiphany while studying in the United States. The puritanical scholar was shocked by Colorado's licentious women, it's true, but more significant was Qutb's encounter with what he later described as America's "evil and fanatic racial discrimination." By coincidence, Qutb arrived in the United States in 1948, the year of the creation of the State of Israel. He witnessed an America blind to the thousands of Palestinians being made permanent refugees by the Zionist project. For Qutb, it wasn't politics, it was an assault on his identity: Clearly Americans believed that Arab lives were worth far less than those of European Jews. According to Yvonne Haddad, a professor of history at Georgetown University, this experience "left Qutb with a bitterness he was never able to shake."

Formative Experiences

When Qutb returned to Egypt he joined the Muslim Brotherhood, leading to his next life-changing event: He was arrested, severely tortured and convicted of antigovernment conspiracy in an absurd show trial. Qutb's political theory was profoundly shaped by torture. Not only did he regard his torturers as subhuman, he stretched that categorization to include the entire state that ordered this brutality, including the practicing Muslims who passively lent their support to [Gamal Abdel] Nasser's regime.

Qutb's vast category of subhumans allowed his disciples to justify the killing of "infidels"—now practically everyone—in the name of Islam. A movement for an Islamic state was transformed into a violent ideology that would lay the intellectual groundwork for Al Qaeda. In other words, so-called Islamist terrorism was "home grown" in the West long before the July 7 [2005 London Transit System] attacks—from its inception it was the quintessentially modern progeny of Colorado's casual racism and Cairo's concentration camps.

Why is it worth digging up this history now? Because the twin sparks that ignited Qutb's world-changing rage are currently being doused with gasoline: Arabs and Muslims are being debased in torture chambers around the world and their deaths are being discounted in simultaneous colonial wars, at the same time that graphic digital evidence of these losses and humiliations is available to anyone with a computer. And once again, this lethal cocktail of racism and torture is burning through the veins of angry young men. As Qutb's past and

Don't Let European Marginalization Infect America

European Muslims and American Muslims have not had much in common until now, but if we unreflectively adopt the European view of Muslims as the perpetual "other," we risk making this true.... Some of our worst laws were passed ... at times of reaction against ethnic communities, from the Palmer Raids of 1919 to today's Patriot Act. In a land founded by immigrants and the rule of law, our nation's strength lies in its resilience; our way of life depends on equal opportunity. Europe and European Muslims are suffering from the inability to bring Muslims into the economic and political mainstream. Will America turn its back on its rich heritage of celebrating diversity?

Moushumi Khan, "The European Problem,"
Slate, July 24, 2007. www.slate.com.

Osman's present reveal, it's not our tolerance for multiculturalism that fuels terrorism; it's our tolerance for the barbarism committed in our name.

Adding Fuel to the Fire

Into this explosive environment has stepped Tony Blair [then British Prime Minister], determined to sell two of the main causes of terror as its cure. He intends to deport more Muslims to countries where they will likely face torture. And he will keep fighting wars in which soldiers don't know the names of the towns they are leveling. (According to an August 5 [2005] Knight Ridder report, a Marine sergeant in Iraq recently pumped up his squad by telling them that "these will be the good old days, when you brought. . .death and destruction to—what the fuck is this place called?" Someone piped in helpfully, "Haqlaniyah.")

Meanwhile, in Britain, there is no shortage of the "evil and fanatic racial discrimination" that Qutb denounced. "Of course too there have been isolated and unacceptable acts of racial or religious hatred," Blair said before unveiling his terror-fighting plan. "But they have been isolated." Isolated? The Islamic Human Rights Commission received 320 complaints of racist attacks in the wake of the bombings; the Monitoring Group has received eighty-three emergency calls; Scotland Yard says hate crimes are up 600 percent from this time last year. Not that pre-July 7 was anything to brag about: "One in five of Britain's ethnic minority voters say that they considered leaving Britain because of racial intolerance," according to a *Guardian* poll in March [2005].

This last statistic shows that the brand of multiculturalism practiced in Britain (and France, Germany, Canada. . .) has little to do with genuine equality. It is instead a Faustian bargain, struck between vote-seeking politicians and self-appointed community leaders, one that keeps ethnic minorities tucked away in state-funded peripheral ghettos while the centers of public life remain largely unaffected by the seismic shifts in the national ethnic makeup. Nothing exposes the shallowness of this alleged tolerance more than the speed with which Muslim communities are now being told to "get out" (to quote Tory MP [Member of Parliament] Gerald Howarth) in the name of core national values.

Integration, Not Ghettoization

The real problem is not too much multiculturalism but too little. If the diversity now ghettoized on the margins of Western societies—geographically and psychologically—were truly allowed to migrate to the centers, it might infuse public life in the West with a powerful new humanism. If we had deeply multi-ethnic societies, rather than shallow multicultural ones, it would be much more difficult for politicians to sign deportation orders sending Algerian asylum-seekers to torture, or to wage wars in which only the invaders' dead are counted. A society that truly lived its values of equality and human rights, at home and abroad, would have another benefit too. It would rob terrorists of what has always been their greatest recruitment tool: our racism.

"Greater technological savvy seems to foster, rather than to diminish, the influence of Eastern delusion."

The Internet Has Encouraged the Growth of Islamic Militancy Among Muslims Living in the West

Feisal G. Mohamed

In this viewpoint, Feisal G. Mohamed, assistant professor of English at the University of Illinois at Urbana-Champaign, argues that the rise in terrorists living in Western societies during the past few years is not sufficiently explained by desperation, inequality, religion, cultural clashes, or foreign policy. He asserts, rather, that the Internet provides immigrants with an instantaneous and constant connection to their homelands, making it much easier to live in a Western culture without assimilating. This not only allows, but also encourages, Muslims living in the West to isolate and identify themselves with Eastern, rather than Western, cultures.

Feisal G. Mohamed, "The Globe of Villages," *Dissent*, Winter 2007, pp. 61–64. www.dissentmagazine.org. Reproduced by permission.

As you read, consider the following questions:

1. Why does Mohamed think that religion, politics, and economics are inadequate explanations for the surge in Western terrorists?

2. What did Marshall McLuhan consider the "cardinal sin of media studies," according to Mohamed?

3. What is wrong with education composed primarily of science and religion, in Mohamed's view?

We have been told that the August 2006 plot to attack several U.S.-bound flights departing from London's Heathrow Airport was hatched largely by Muslim Britons. This is becoming a familiar story. Earlier this summer [June 2006], the Royal Canadian Mounted Police foiled a home-grown Toronto cell in its attempt to blow up Parliament with a fertilizer bomb similar to that used by Timothy McVeigh in the [April 1995] Oklahoma City bombing. The July 7, 2005, attacks on London buses and subways were carried out largely by British citizens, and this was not the first such occurrence: two Britons traveled to Tel Aviv in 2003 to conduct a suicide bombing of a nightclub that killed three and wounded sixty.

This country too has produced its share of accused or convicted jihadists. The "Lackawanna Six," all American citizens of Yemeni heritage, were arrested in 2002 for attending an al-Qaeda camp in Afghanistan—much like Hamid Hayat, a second-generation Pakistani-American, who was convicted last year, albeit on dubious evidence, for receiving jihadist training in Pakistan. Iyman Faris, an American citizen born in Kashmir, was sentenced to twenty years in prison in 2005 for participating in a plan to attack the Brooklyn Bridge. These men are joined by several other Americans who have been found guilty of providing material or logistic support to Islamist terrorists: Marwan Othman el-Hindi, Uzair Paracha, Junaid Babar, and Ali al-Timimi and his "Virginia jihadists." I say nothing of the Miami "cell" arrested in June 2006 for conspiring with al-Qaeda, whose members seemed more interested in using terrorist funds to buy a new wardrobe than in waging holy war; or of Naveed Haq, whose attack on a Jewish community center in Seattle this August [2006] killed one and injured five (it has been suggested that he acted entirely on his own and has a history of mental illness); nor am I concerned with such converts as José Padilla, Richard Reid, and the three recently arrested [August 2006] in connection with the attempt to explode passenger jets over the Atlantic: Don Stewart-Whyte, Brian Young, and Oliver Savant. (One wonders if these men turned to violence after converting to Islam or if they converted to Islam so that they might engage in spectacular anti-Western violence.)

Inadequate Explanations

As yet we have not been offered a satisfactory explanation of this political or religious zealotry. The terms by which foreign terrorism is made scrutable are quite familiar by now: faced with a lack of opportunity in the Arab world and the humiliations—real and imagined—dealt to one's coreligionists, desperate youth come to see themselves as engaged in cosmic warfare against iniquity and turn to violence. In this vein, Mohammed Atta, the ringleader of the September 11 [2001] attacks, is held up as the paradigmatic modern terrorist. Despite his education and residence in Germany, he became hostile toward the West upon return to his native Egypt, where his world-class training as an engineer fitted him only for unemployment, and where he saw the birthplace of one of the world's great civilizations reduced to a satrapy prostrating itself before the Western tourist dollar. Such a narrative of the development of a terrorist has provided comfort in the West across the political spectrum. The conservative finds in it an irreconcilable clash of civilizations: no matter how much we give to these people they still hate us; best to have a firm hand. The liberal finds in it evidence of universal outrage over the evils of global capitalism and American foreign policy: if Western industry, and particularly big oil, had a shred of regard for the prosperity of the Arab majority, if the United States did not prop up Arab tyrants and simultaneously inflict suffering on the Palestinians and Iraqis, there would be no terrorists.

But the phenomenon of Western jihadists is harder to explain than this suggests. If religion is the explanation for terrorism—if we argue that Iran and Saudi Arabia have used their oil wealth to assure the global spread of retrograde ideas in both of Islam's major sects, so that each one now strives to outdo the other in paranoia—we still cannot entirely explain why lunatic Muslim clerics have found an audience among young men born into liberal societies. And if politics and economics are the explanation for terrorism, why is it that those who are stakeholders in affluent Western democracies feel directly involved in political struggles taking place on the other side of the planet?

Greater Sense of Unity

The real question is, what makes the religion and politics of radical Islam seem to apply to the situation of a Muslim in London, Toronto, or Brooklyn? This is not the same as the question that is often identified as pressing: whether Muslim immigrants in the West are assimilating into the host culture.

Many immigrant communities show little regard for assimilation. Any walk through a self-respecting Chinatown, for example, will reveal a significant number of individuals making a life in the West that is culturally closer to the motherland than to their adopted home. Those who clamor for fuller assimilation of Muslims reveal their discomfort with the increasingly multicultural complexion of the West in a way only tangentially related to this particular minority group; they use terrorism as a cover for their dislike of foreign dress, beliefs, and manners. Nor can the isolation of the Muslim community—imposed from within and without—be regarded as the key motivation for violence. Isolation has always been, and ever will be, a condition of immigrant life, and there are many fewer obstacles faced by Muslims today than have been peacefully overcome by the Asian, Jewish, Irish, Italian, Mexican, Native, and African Americans who have suffered most in the long and continuing struggle to broaden this country's promise of dignity and prosperity.

Present-day conditions of immigration do seem, however, to foster an especially keen sense of unity between diaspora and kin country. The first such condition is the mobility of the modern world, which produces a constant state of traffic between East and West. Rather than arrival en masse and slow adaptation, the modern immigrant community is in a state of constant exchange with the mother country. Those who immigrate will travel home regularly; many who reside in the West will do so temporarily; this allows cultural and emotional bonds with non-Western society to remain firmly intact.

A New Source of Ideas

The exchange of people across East and West, however, may not be as important as it seems at first glance. Even the influence of itinerant Muslim preachers may not be as decisive as it looks. A good deal has been done, in England especially, to crack down on radical clerics; perhaps that country has learned the lesson of its seventeenth-century civil wars, fired as they were from the Puritan pulpit. But a recent survey by the Federation of Student Islamic Societies suggests that the vast majority of young British Muslims get their ideas outside of the mosque. The underground meeting and the Web site are the crucial milieus of the radical subculture.

It is the means by which ideas, rather than people, are exchanged that is the real issue, and especially the way in which modern communications make it possible to identify exclusively with one's kin country while living elsewhere.

One of the consequences of the Internet is its generation of communities of readers without geographical association. As a technology bound to the distribution of physical objects, the printed page necessarily reflects the values of a given locale. If we were still shackled to print—and I mean the cast-metal-striking-paper kind, not the ink or laser jet variety—the cost of delivering al-Qaeda propaganda to East London would be prohibitive; the lack of broad demand would make it a hopeless venture. The dissemination of ideas on the Web is not married to the local market; once one has a functioning computer and an active Internet connection, it is just as easy to access al-Jazeera as it is FoxNews. The market forces governing such access have shifted profoundly, so that where one lives is no longer an index of what one reads or thinks. This may be why a recent Pew study found that many of the most obnoxious ideas of the Arab world are alive and well in Europe: for example, 56 percent of the British Muslims surveyed claimed that Arabs did not carry out the September 11 attacks, as compared to 53 percent in Jordan, 41 percent in Pakistan, and 47 percent in Nigeria. This may also be why many young Muslims born and raised in the West are more radical in their religious views than their parents are. Greater technological savvy seems to foster, rather than to diminish, the influence of Eastern delusion.

A Mystique of Participation

What I am suggesting here goes beyond the now-redundant claim that the Internet has been an important means by which Islamism organizes itself. As the *Washington Post* observed in August 2005, attacks on al-Qaeda camps in Afghanistan have led to the creation of virtual training facilities. "To join the great training camps you don't have to travel to other lands," one Saudi magazine claims, "alone, in your home or with a

The Internet and a Globalized Islam

Olivier Roy—The Internet is a perfect tool to create an abstract and virtual community of believers delinked from any specific country and culture. The sites are either in English or Arabic, the links refer to a corpus of contemporary thinkers (most of them Salafis, by the way). . . .

Moreover, the Internet allows an individual to speak on an equal footing with others. There is no hierarchy of knowledge. . . . It is a kind of religious free market, where one can shop for very different products, from fatwas to cooking recipes or matrimonial advice, without leaving one's room.

Jean-Francois Mayer, Interview with Olivier Roy, Religioscope, Nov. 8, 2004. www.religion.info.

group of your brothers, you too can begin to execute the training program." Michael Dartnell's recent book *Insurgency Online* shows how the Internet has allowed non-state actors to achieve new levels of organization and thus to exert previously unimaginable political influence. Even [U.S. Department of Homeland Security Secretary] Michael Chertoff has emerged from the Department of Homeland Security's thick cloud of bureaucracy to shed some light on this front, claiming in a recent issue of the *Atlantic Monthly*, that "we have to look at the onset of virtual terrorism—virtual jihad—where groups radicalize themselves over the Internet."

The shortcoming of such commentary is that it commits what [educator and communications theorist] Marshall McLuhan described as the cardinal sin of media studies: it focuses on content rather than on the medium itself. We miss the point in claiming that the jihadists are visiting the wrong Web sites. What is really significant is that the Internet has made it possible for new human relationships to emerge. "The medium is the message," in McLuhan's famous phrase, "because it is the medium that shapes and controls the scale and form of human association and action."

It is a commonplace of cultural history to say that vernacular print and its reading public helped to create the idea of the modern nation-state. Electronic communications are causing this idea to dissolve. Individuals are led into a mystique of participation in affairs across the globe, from one laptop in East London to another in the mountains outside of Jalalabad. And in electronic media this mystique of participation is the end itself, rather than argument and explanation. No longer is society bound by the rational interpretation of the physical and social world that print generates—the anvil on which the liberal tradition was forged. Instead it is being rent asunder as various groups are drawn to the visceral totems of image-based media. Though McLuhan thought that the sense of universal participation generated by electronic media would put an end to parochialism, quite the opposite has occurred. Rather than his global village, we have become a globe of villages; we live in a cacophony of hidebound parochialisms where individuals seek association only with those to whom they relate by way of primordial intuition.

Unexpected Proximity

McLuhan may have been correct to say that the most "backward," the least literate parts of the world would take up the new media most eagerly, but he did not foresee the conflicts that the new media might create within a multicultural West. The liberal state, with its dependence on rational association, is dissolving into a collection of masses united by the parochialisms of "religion" and "culture," a phenomenon to be observed among Muslims and non-Muslims alike.

Can a little Internet surfing really do all that? Yes, and to illustrate why it is so, allow me a moment of autobiography. I was once reading a Philip Roth novel and came across the phrase, "Newark was all of Jewry to me"—I can't remember which one it was; it could have been any of Roth's works. This single statement made me realize more about my own ethnicity than any other I have encountered before or since. As with Roth, everything I had grown up recognizing as a part of my ethnic heritage—Egyptians don't play sports, drink, or curse; they wear their religion lightly, laugh from the soul, and are moved to outrage only when their children underachieve at school—had been learned from the hundred or so households of Egyptian emigrés in my hometown of Edmonton, Canada, nearly all of whom, men and women, I proudly stress, were university-educated professionals. Only after reading Roth's statement did it occur to me that though I had always identified myself as Egyptian-Canadian, my sense of what was Egyptian had little connection to the seventy-two million individuals living a world away in Egypt, most of whom eke out a subsistence living using agricultural techniques that have not changed in the past millennium.

At the same moment, I saw that my sense of identity was very much like that of an author with whom it should be doubly antithetical: he being a Jewish American and I a Muslim Canadian. And recognizing this unexpected proximity made me realize that a minority experience much like my own had found its way into the mainstream of North American life. This led me along a chain of ideas to the point with which I began this essay: that isolation has always been, and always will be, a condition of immigrant life.

Literacy and Connection

But had I grown up in the age of the blogosphere, I might have found a radically different narrative by which to explain my minority experience. If I had spent my time surfing the

Net rather than reading novels, I might have been more prone to isolate myself with my coreligionists rather than to see myself as having a specifically Western experience of the world. This is also the great irony that homegrown jihadists fail to see: though they may feel a mystique of participation with the plight of Muslims on the other side of the planet, it is only a mystique. Looking at their blogs shows just how thoroughly their lives and hopes partake in the Western version of self-indulgent, egocentric adolescence. Toronto's *Globe and Mail* has provided a look at the blog of Zakaria Amara, leader of that city's homegrown jihadists, which reveals this sensibility: underneath the Islamist rhetoric one finds a teenager confused by his raging hormones, convinced that the older generation has accepted a corrupt world and fallen into lethargic inaction—and anxious over college applications. Had he been reading Roth rather than the ravings of zealots to which the Internet provides too-ready access, he might have found quite a different sympathetic voice to help him make sense of himself and the world around him.

This is not to say that current efforts to crack down on radical Islam are entirely misguided. No civil society should tolerate a cleric who advocates its destruction and incites his listeners to do the necessary work. The move in Britain to observe mosques and to expel radical imams is entirely appropriate. But if Western Muslims are to carve out their own identity as other minorities have done—neither "assimilated" nor clinging to the bigotries of the motherland—the brand of identity to which electronic media contribute must also be addressed. A robust censorship of radical Web sites would only address content; we also need to promote real literacy and the concomitant primacy of reason. If the new vogue for religion-based schooling is allowed to flourish, it must force students to become "people of the book," to use the Prophet Muhammad's phrase. Emphasizing only science and religion, with little regard for a humanities curriculum of literature and history, creates an intellectual environment where parochialism flourishes.

It is through literacy that we become rational observers of both West and East, and it is through literacy that Muslims can reclaim the long intellectual and artistic traditions that have been occluded by the rise in the twentieth century of Saudi Wahhabism, Iranian radical Shiism, and the Arab world's histrionic opposition to the state of Israel. Only then will Muslims themselves tear the veil of false holiness off a radical Islam that is itself a cover for the political tyrannies of today's Middle East.

> *"This is not a clash between civiliza-*
> *tions; it is a clash about civilization. It*
> *is the age-old battle between progress*
> *and reaction."*

Islamic Militancy Is a Rejection of Western Values

Tony Blair

In this viewpoint, British Prime Minister Tony Blair (in office from 1997 to June 2007) argues that Islamic militancy is not driven by religion, poverty or injustice. Rather, it is an advancement of a set of values in direct conflict with Western values of democracy, tolerance, and liberty. Therefore, Blair asserts, such militancy can only be effectively defeated by convincing all people that Western values are superior to those of the terrorists. Beyond just fighting terrorists, the West must unite the world around solving global issues, including conflict in the Middle East, poverty, and climate change.

As you read, consider the following questions:

1. In Blair's view, what is the extremists' goal in Iraq and Afghanistan?
2. What is the danger of the United States, according to Blair?

Tony Blair, "A Battle for Global Values," *Foreign Affairs*, vol. 86, no. 1, January/February 2007. www.foreignaffairs.org. Reproduced by permission of the publisher.

3. Why does Blair think a Middle East peace settlement would disprove Islamic militant ideology?

Our response to the September 11, [2001] attacks has proved even more momentous than it seemed at the time. That is because we could have chosen security as the battleground. But we did not. We chose values. We said that we did not want another Taliban or a different Saddam Hussein. We knew that you cannot defeat a fanatical ideology just by imprisoning or killing its leaders; you have to defeat its ideas.

In my view, the situation we face is indeed war, but of a completely unconventional kind, one that cannot be won in a conventional way. We will not win the battle against global extremism unless we win it at the level of values as much as that of force. We can win only by showing that our values are stronger, better, and more just than the alternative. That also means showing the world that we are evenhanded and fair in our application of those values. We will never get real support for the tough actions that may well be essential to safeguarding our way of life unless we also attack global poverty, environmental degradation, and injustice with equal vigor.

The roots of the current wave of global terrorism and extremism are deep. They reach down through decades of alienation, victimhood, and political oppression in the Arab and Muslim world. Yet such terrorism is not and never has been inevitable.

To me, the most remarkable thing about the Koran is how progressive it is. I write with great humility as a member of another faith. As an outsider, the Koran strikes me as a reforming book, trying to return Judaism and Christianity to their origins, much as reformers attempted to do with the Christian church centuries later. The Koran is inclusive. It extols science and knowledge and abhors superstition. It is practical and far ahead of its time in attitudes toward marriage, women, and governance.

Under its guidance, the spread of Islam and its dominance over previously Christian or pagan lands were breathtaking. Over centuries, Islam founded an empire and led the world in discovery, art, and culture. The standard-bearers of tolerance in the early Middle Ages were far more likely to be found in Muslim lands than in Christian ones.

The Beginnings of Extremist Ideology

But by the early twentieth century, after the Renaissance, the Reformation, and the Enlightenment had swept over the Western world, the Muslim and Arab world was uncertain, insecure, and on the defensive. Some Muslim countries, such as Turkey, made a muscular move toward secularism [an indifference to or rejection of religion and religious considerations]. Others found themselves caught up in colonization, nascent nationalism, political oppression, and religious radicalism. Muslims began to see the sorry state of Muslim countries as symptomatic of the sorry state of Islam. Political radicals became religious radicals and vice versa.

Those in power tried to accommodate this Islamic radicalism by incorporating some of its leaders and some of its ideology. The result was nearly always disastrous. Religious radicalism was made respectable and political radicalism suppressed, and so in the minds of many, the two came together to represent the need for change. They began to think that the way to restore the confidence and stability of Islam was through a combination of religious extremism and populist politics, with the enemies becoming "the West" and those Islamic leaders who cooperated with it.

This extremism may have started with religious doctrine and thought. But soon, in offshoots of the Muslim Brotherhood, supported by Wahhabi extremists and disseminated in some of the madrasahs of the Middle East and Asia, an ideology was born and exported around the world.

On 9/11, 3,000 people were murdered. But this terrorism did not begin on the streets of New York. Many more had already died, not just in acts of terrorism against Western interests but in political insurrection and turmoil around the world. Its victims are to be found in the recent history of many lands: India, Indonesia, Kenya, Libya, Pakistan, Russia, Saudi Arabia, Yemen, and countless more. More than 100,000 died in Algeria. In Chechnya and Kashmir, political causes that could have been resolved became brutally incapable of resolution under the pressure of terrorism. Today, in 30 or 40 countries, terrorists are plotting action loosely linked with this ideology. Although the active cadres of terrorists are relatively small, they exploit a far wider sense of alienation in the Arab and Muslim world.

Muslims Versus the West

These acts of terrorism were not isolated incidents. They were part of a growing movement—a movement that believed Muslims had departed from their proper faith, were being taken over by Western culture, and were being governed treacherously by Muslims complicit in this takeover (as opposed to those who could see that the way to recover not just the true faith but also Muslim confidence and self-esteem was to take on the West and all its works).

The struggle against terrorism in Madrid, or London, or Paris is the same as the struggle against the terrorist acts of Hezbollah in Lebanon, or Palestinian Islamic Jihad in the Palestinian territories, or rejectionist groups in Iraq. The murder of the innocent in Beslan [, Russia] is part of the same ideology that takes innocent lives in Libya, Saudi Arabia, or Yemen. And when Iran gives support to such terrorism, it becomes part of the same battle, with the same ideology at its heart.

Sometimes political strategy comes deliberatively, sometimes by instinct. For this movement, it probably came by instinct. It has an ideology, a worldview, deep convictions, and the determination of fanaticism. It resembles, in many ways, early revolutionary communism. It does not always need structures and command centers or even explicit communication. It knows what it thinks.

In the late 1900s, the movement's strategy became clear. If it was merely fighting within Islam, it ran the risk that fellow Muslims—being as decent and as fair-minded as anyone else— would choose to reject its fanaticism. A battle about Islam was just Muslim versus Muslim. The extremists realized that they had to create a completely different battle: Muslims versus the West.

That is what the September 11 attacks did. I am still amazed at how many people say, in effect, that there is terrorism today because of the invasions of Afghanistan and Iraq. They seem to forget entirely that 9/11 predated both. The West did not attack this movement. It was attacked.

The Nature of the Struggle

For this ideology, we are the enemy. But "we" are not the West. "We" are as much Muslim as Christian, Jew, or Hindu. "We" are all those who believe in religious tolerance, in openness to others, in democracy, in liberty, and in human rights administered by secular courts.

This is not a clash between civilizations; it is a clash about civilization. It is the age-old battle between progress and reaction, between those who embrace the modern world and those who reject its existence—between optimism and hope, on the one hand, and pessimism and fear, on the other.

In any struggle, the first challenge is to accurately perceive the nature of what is being fought over, and here we have a long way to go. It is almost incredible to me that so much Western opinion appears to buy the idea that the emergence of this global terrorism is somehow our fault.

For a start, the terror is truly global. It is directed not just at the United States and its allies but also at nations who could not conceivably be said to be partners of the West.

Moreover, the struggles in Iraq and Afghanistan are plainly not about those countries' liberation from U.S. occupation. The extremists' goal is to prevent those countries from becoming democracies—not "Western-style" democracies but any sort of democracy. It is the extremists, not us, who are slaughtering the innocent and doing it deliberately. They are the only reason for the continuing presence of our troops in Iraq and Afghanistan.

Erroneous Explanations

It is also rubbish to suggest that Islamist terrorism is the product of poverty. Of course, it uses the cause of poverty as a justification for its acts. But its fanatics are hardly champions of economic development.

Furthermore, the terrorists' aim is not to encourage the creation of a Palestine living side by side with Israel but rather to prevent it. They fight not for the coming into being of a Palestinian state but for the going out of being of an Israeli state. The terrorists base their ideology on religious extremism—and not just any religious extremism, but a specifically Muslim version. The terrorists do not want Muslim countries to modernize. They hope that the arc of extremism that now stretches across the region will sweep away the fledgling but faltering steps modern Islam wants to take into the future. They want the Muslim world to retreat into governance by a semifeudal religious oligarchy.

Yet despite all of this, which I consider fairly obvious, many in Western countries listen to the propaganda of the extremists and accept it. (And to give credit where it is due, the extremists play our own media with a shrewdness that would be the envy of many a political party.) They look at the bloodshed in Iraq and say it is a reason for leaving. Every act of

Our Values Are Their Targets

Even a perfunctory look at the core beliefs of Islamism—as expressed in the writings of its leading ideologues—is enough to realize that it is our liberal civilization and its norms of freedom, democracy, secularism, and human rights that are the main enemy and target of the Islamofascists. It is these values Islamist sermons in mosques around the world urge Muslims to conduct jihad against and destroy. And those of us who believe in these values, Muslim and non-Muslim alike, ipso facto become apostates, deviants, and infidels, a category of subhumans whose blood can readily be spilled.

Alex Alexiev, "What It Takes," National Review, *Nov. 7, 2005.*

carnage somehow serves to indicate our responsibility for the disorder rather than the wickedness of those who caused it. Many believe that what was done in Iraq in 2003 was so wrong that they are reluctant to accept what is plainly right now.

Ideas Must Be Confronted as Well

Some people believe that terrorist attacks are caused entirely by the West's suppression of Muslims. Some people seriously believe that if we only got out of Iraq and Afghanistan, the attacks would stop. And, in some ways most perniciously [destructive], many look at Israel and think we pay too great a price for supporting it and sympathize with those who condemn it.

If we recognized this struggle for what it truly is, we would at least be on the first steps of the path to winning it. But a vast part of Western opinion is not remotely near this point yet.

This ideology has to be taken on—and taken on everywhere. Islamist terrorism will not be defeated until we confront not just the methods of the extremists but also their ideas. I do not mean just telling them that terrorist activity is wrong. I mean telling them that their attitude toward the United States is absurd, that their concept of governance is prefeudal, that their positions on women and other faiths are reactionary. We must reject not just their barbaric acts but also their false sense of grievance against the West, their attempt to persuade us that it is others and not they themselves who are responsible for their violence.

In the era of globalization, the outcome of this clash between extremism and progress will determine our future. We can no more opt out of this struggle than we can opt out of the climate changing around us. Inaction—pushing the responsibility onto the United States alone or deluding ourselves that this terrorism is a series of individual isolated incidents rather than a global movement—would be profoundly and fundamentally wrong. . . .

The Battle for Hearts and Minds

This is ultimately a battle about modernity. Some of it can be conducted and won only within Islam itself. But let us remember that extremism is not the true voice of Islam. Millions of Muslims the world over want what all people want: to be free and for others to be free. They regard tolerance as a virtue and respect for the faith of others as a part of their own faith.

This is a battle of values and for progress, and therefore it is one that must be won. If we want to secure our way of life, there is no alternative but to fight for it. That means standing up for our values, not just in our own countries but the world over. We need to construct a global alliance for these global values and act through it. Inactivity is just as much a policy, with its own results. It is simply the wrong one.

Islamist extremism's whole strategy is based on a presumed sense of grievance that divides people against one another. Our answer has to be a set of values strong enough to unite people with one another. This is not just about security or military tactics. It is about hearts and minds, about inspiring people, persuading them, showing them what our values stand for at their best. Why are we not yet succeeding? Because we are not being bold enough, consistent enough, thorough enough in fighting for the values we believe in.

Simply to state it in these terms is to underline how much has to be done. Convincing Western publics of the nature of the battle is hard enough. But we then have to empower modern, moderate, mainstream forces in the Islamic world to defeat their reactionary opponents.

We have to show that our values are not Western, still less American or Anglo-Saxon, but values in the common ownership of humanity, universal values that should be the right of the global citizen.

We Must Be Persuasive

Ranged against us are people who truly hate us. But beyond them are many more who do not hate us but do question our motives, good faith, and evenhandedness. These are people who could support our values but who believe we ourselves support them only selectively. These are the people we must persuade. They have to know this is about justice and fairness as well as security and prosperity.

That is why on a whole range of critical issues, we face not just powerful questions about our national interests but also vital tests of our commitment to global values. If we believe in justice, how can we let 30,000 children a day die when those deaths could be prevented? If we believe in our responsibility to the generations that come after us, how can we be indifferent to the degradation of the planet? How can we have a global trading system based on unfair trade? How can we bring peace to the Middle East unless we resolve the question of Israel and Palestine?

Wherever people live in fear, with no prospect of advance, we should be on their side, in solidarity with them, whether in Myanmar, North Korea, Sudan, or Zimbabwe. Wherever countries are in the process of democratic development, we should extend a helping hand.

This requires, across the board, an active foreign policy of engagement, not isolation. And it cannot be achieved without a strong alliance, with the United States and Europe at its core. The necessary alliance does not end there, but it does begin there.

Let me be quite plain here. I do not always agree with the United States. Sometimes it can be a difficult friend to have. But the strain of anti-American feeling in parts of Europe is madness when set against the long-term interests of the world we believe in. The danger with the United States today is not that it is too involved in the world. The danger is that it might pull up the drawbridge and disengage. The world needs it involved. The world wants it engaged. The reality is that none of the problems that press in on us can be resolved or even approached without it.

Beyond Security

The challenge now is to ensure that the agenda is not limited to security alone. There is a danger of a division of global politics into "hard" and "soft," with the "hard" efforts going after the terrorists, whereas the "soft" campaign focuses on poverty and injustice. That divide is dangerous because interdependence makes all these issues just that: interdependent. The answer to terrorism is the universal application of global values; the answer to poverty and injustice is the same. That is why the struggle for global values has to be applied not selectively but to the whole global agenda.

We need to reenergize the peace process between Israel and the Palestinians—and we need to do so in a dramatic and profound manner. Its significance for the broader issue of the Middle East and for the battle within Islam goes beyond correcting the plight of the Palestinians. A settlement would be the living, visible proof that the region and the world can accommodate different faiths and cultures. It would not only silence reactionary Islam's most effective rallying call but fatally undermine its basic ideology.

We must combat the ravages of poverty, famine, disease, and conflict, particularly in Africa, increasing our aid still further and stepping up our activity. Before the United Kingdom's presidency of the G-8, the group of leading industrial powers, in 2005, the issues of Africa and climate change were not high on the political agenda in London, let alone internationally. Now they are. This is due in no small part to the efforts of millions of people energized by the Make Poverty History campaign and Live 8 [a string of benefit concerts that took place in July 2005, the goal of which was to alleviate poverty in the world's poorest nations], which played an extraordinary part in mobilizing civil society. But just because the issues are at the top of the agenda now does not mean that they cannot easily slip down again.

We must ensure that they do not. We must continue to mobilize the resources and the will to turn the commitments of 2005 into action. I have seen that if there is real commitment by African governments to progress, then the people of Africa are quite capable of doing the rest. Which is why, no matter how desperate the situation looks or how insurmountable the obstacles appear, we have to maintain optimism that progress is indeed possible.

Focus on Solving Global Problems

We need to jump-start talks on trade. At stake, obviously, is our commitment to fighting world poverty and supporting development. But also in the balance is the very idea of using multilateral action to achieve common goals. If we cannot conduct a decent trade round, when it is so plain that our long-term national interests and the wider interests of the world demand it, this will be a failure with multiple consequences, all of them adverse. Europe's agricultural protection is a policy born of another age, and it is time to end it. But change in Europe alone is not the answer. The United States must also open up. Japan, too. In improving access to nonagricultural markets, we look to leadership from Brazil and India. And we must agree on a development package for the poorest that includes 100 percent market access and aid for trade.

Finally, the whole world needs to focus on the threat of climate change. Future generations will not forgive us if we do not pay attention to the degrading and polluting of our planet. We need a clear, disciplined framework for action, with measurable outcomes that all the major players buy into and that has at its heart the goal to stabilize greenhouse gas concentrations and the planet's temperature. I believe a clear goal and a strong framework would help spur the technology revolution we need. It is vital to give business the certainty it requires to invest in cleaner technology and reduce emissions.

The United States wants a low-carbon economy; it is investing heavily in clean technology; it needs China and India to grow substantially. The world is ready for a new start. Washington can help lead it.

Let Our Values Guide Us

In my nine years as prime minister, I have not become less idealistic or more cynical. I have simply become more persuaded that the distinction between a foreign policy driven by values and one driven by interests is wrong. Globalization begets interdependence, and interdependence begets the necessity of a common value system to make it work. Idealism thus becomes realpolitik.

None of this eliminates the setbacks, shortfalls, inconsistencies, and hypocrisies that come with practical decision-making in a harsh world. But it does mean that the best of the human spirit, which has pushed the progress of humanity along, is also the best hope for the world's future.

That is why I say this struggle is one about values. Our values are our guide. They represent humanity's progress throughout the ages. At each point we have had to fight for them and defend them. As a new age beckons, it is time to fight for them again.

"Islamistic anti-Semitism sees the fight against the Jews as the first and central piece in their program."

Islamic Militancy Is Another Manifestation of Anti-Semitism

Yehuda Bauer

In this viewpoint, Yehuda Bauer discusses the many manifestations of anti-Semitism. He argues that anti-Semitism is not always rooted in economic hardship, and that cultural, political, and theological factors also may be causes. According to the author, anti-Semitism has been a part of radical Islamist ideology since the 1920s; therefore, the Israeli-Palestinian conflict is not the root of this relationship. Further, because radical Islamist philosophy regards Jews as symbolic leaders of the West, their annihilation is a crucial goal of that movement. Yehuda Bauer is professor emeritus of Holocaust Studies at the Hebrew University and the author of several books, including Rethinking the Holocaust.

Yehuda Bauer, "Beyond the Fourth Wave: Contemporary Anti-Semitism and Radical Islam," *Judaism: A Quarterly Journal of Jewish Life and Thought*, vol. 55, nos. 1–2, Fall 2006, pp. 55–62. Copyright © 2006 American Jewish Congress. Reproduced by permission.

As you read, consider the following questions:

1. According to Bauer, when did the fourth wave of anti-Semitism begin?
2. How are Jews described in the Qur'an, according to Bauer?
3. What is one characteristic that distinguishes radical Islam from Nazism and Communism, in Bauer's view?

The term "anti-semitism," as many of us realize, is the wrong term for what we try to describe and analyze. It is inane nonsense, because there is no "Semitism" one can be "anti" to. There are Semitic languages, and you can hardly be against Semitic languages. We have come to use "anti-Semitism" to describe dislike of Jews—and worse.

In reality, the term fits only Jew-hatred . . . (*sinat yisrael*) from about the middle of the 19th century onward. Even then, the mixture of Christian and Muslim theological opposition to Jews, traditional economic jealousy and competitiveness, and racial-biological and nationalistic ideological motives make it difficult to encompass all that with this essentially erroneous term. It makes a mess of research projects, as it interferes with the task of differentiation. Yet we all use it, simply because we have not come up with the proper terminology. So, knowing we are talking nonsense when we use it, let us use it, *faute de mieux* [for lack of a better word].

Since 1945, there have been three waves of anti-Semitism (I prefer to spell it as one word, a translation of the original Antisemitismus, but that is not the style here) and we are now experiencing a fourth. The approximate dates are 1958–1960, 1968–1972, and 1987–1992, with the fourth wave beginning in 1999 or 2000. An analysis done in Jerusalem by Simcha Epstein has shown that the motivations were different in each case and, in the third, the one beginning in 1987, no economic motivation has been shown. That means that our traditional explanations that modern anti-Semitism always has something to do with economic downturns are inaccurate. It seems that cultural, political, economic or theological crises can all be causes, or part causes, of a phenomenon that cannot be explained monocausally.

At the basis is the fact that the Jews produced a civilization that differed in some central aspects from the civilizations around them. Jews were certainly no better or worse than others, but they were different in the way they conducted their lives. Had they stayed in their hilly land, they would have been another interesting and peculiar tribe; but they spread, more by conversion than expulsion. The Jews carried their distinctive civilization with them everywhere they went, and it marked them off against their environment.

Theological Sources

Crises of whatever source could, and sometimes did, cause this basically defenseless, well-known yet strange minority to be seen as the reason for the crisis and, therefore, Jews were subject to discrimination or attack. [sinat yisrael] is the oldest group hatred that exists; it precedes racism, because as we know, blacks who acknowledged Roman gods and were free men could—and did—become Roman citizens of equal status. Jews were intensely disliked: They refused to acknowledge the gods; they would not share meals with their neighbors; and on the whole they kept themselves separate. This solidified in the theological power dispute with Christianity and, later, Islam. The economic stresses came later and, contrary to Marxist interpretations, they were the result of the theological tensions, not the other way round.

This Christian theological basis is today slowly being eroded. Christian churches are gradually developing the idea that there may be several ways to serve God, and that theirs may not be the only one. In the struggle against contemporary anti-Semitism, the Christian churches are often allies, not opponents.

However, many hundreds of years of an anti-Semitic culture have had their result in the formation of an underlying latency of anti-Semitism that waits to explode when aroused by some outside crisis. In the post-Holocaust era, this has been complicated by two major events of a political and cultural nature: the Shoah [Holocaust] and the establishment of the State of Israel.

The Holocaust created an unease about the Jews, especially in Europe, where people have to live with nearly Six Million ghosts, created by a deadly mutation of European culture. As the famous saying goes—the Europeans, and not necessarily only the Germans, cannot forgive the Jews for Auschwitz [the largest Nazi concentration camp]. Periods of self-accusation and beating of breasts alternate with periods in which everything is done to turn the Jews into perpetrators—nowadays, even into Nazis—in order to liberate the heirs of European culture from the burden of the genocide.

Nationalistic Conflicts

The establishment of Israel caused a widespread feeling of relief for the Europeans on the one hand: "We do not have to bother about the Jews anymore, they have made good, they are wonderful, they will create a new Christianity for us, or a new socialism—a humanistic, idealistic society that will bring salvation to a sick world." On the other hand, Israel turned the victims into perpetrators; David became Goliath and, when occasion arose, everything was—and is—done to identify Israel with evil. Either way, Israel is singled out, a collective deity or an evil force.

The Arab-Israeli conflict, and now the Israeli-Palestinian confrontation, provide ample material for an anti-Semitism that sees itself as anti-Zionist [against the establishment of Israel as a Jewish nation], rather than anti-Jewish. Indeed, in theory at least, one can be anti-Zionist without being anti-Semitic, but only if one believes that all national movements are evil and that all national states should be abolished. If one argues, however, that the Fijians have a right to independence, and so do the Malays and the Bolivians, but not the Jews, then one is anti-Jewish. As one singles out the Jews for nationalistic reasons, one is anti-Semitic, with an attendant strong suspicion of being racist.

There is just cause to criticize Israel at times. It is, after all, locked in a bitter struggle with a Palestinian nationalism that is no less legitimate than its own. It often must react to Palestinian terrorism in ways that cause serious violations of human rights and terrible suffering to human beings. However, anti-Semitic latency in the West latches on to that tragic dispute so as to brand the Jews as mass murderers and Nazis, in order to solve the social psychological problem caused by the Holocaust.

It appears that the current fourth wave of anti-Semitism since 1945 is a basically upper middle class, intellectual phenomenon in the West. It is widespread in the media, in universities and in well-manicured circles. Its manifestations are not important; what matters are *that* it exists and *where* it exists.

One should not generalize, however. Many Europeans, and most Americans—especially of the working and middle classes, but also among the elites—are opposed to the re-emerging anti-Semitism. I believe this wave will pass in time.

The Danger of Radical Islam

On the whole, it is not Western anti-Semitism, with all its dangers, that causes me to worry, but something else: Islamic radicalism.

Radical Islam is a developing ideology and it fuels international terrorism. Rarely do people ask what are the aims of that ideology, where it comes from, what is the historical context that made it grow, and how widespread it is. The usual response to it is that it should be rooted out and destroyed. Is force, however, the only correct answer?

Most people refer to radical Islam as being fundamentalist, yet its outstanding features go far beyond fundamentalism.

One has to say, first of all, that Islam and radical Islam are not necessarily the same thing—although many experts of Islam will disagree with this statement. What does radical Islam believe in, and what is the difference between it and non-radical Islam? The crucial, central element in radical Islam is the conviction that Western civilization has passed its peak, that it is declining into corruption and weakness, and that the future lies with radical Islam. The aim, says radical Islamic ideology, must be the conquest of the whole world and the acceptance of Islam by the conquered.

The second element is the desire to abolish politics as such. God-Allah has told the world, through His prophet, how men should govern themselves and what laws they should follow. Any human intervention, whether through parliamentary democracy or through any type of autocracy, is blasphemy. The world will be run by men trained in Islamic law, and national and territorial boundaries will be simply a matter of convenience.

Hence also comes the third point: Radical Islam aspires to the abolition of national states, first and foremost Arab national states. Thus, Hamas and Islamic Jihad in Gaza and on the West Bank do not demand a Palestinian national state, but an Islamic state of Palestine, which will be almost as anti-Christian as it will be anti-Jewish.

Radical Islamic Ideology

Finally, radical Islam is at the same time a utopian and an apocalyptic ideology. It promises a wonderful, peaceful world, ruled by God Himself, through Islam, and thus aspires to the end of history as we know it—because obviously, there can be no history after the establishment of the rule of God. I have

The Koran's Anti-Semitism

The Koran's overall discussion of the Jews is marked by a litany of their sins and punishments, as if part of a divine indictment, conviction, and punishment process. The Jews wronged themselves (16:118) by losing faith (7:168) and breaking their covenant (5:13). The Jews . . . are a nation that has passed away (2:134; repeated in 2:141). Twice Allah sent his instruments (the Assyrians/or Babylonians, and Romans) to punish this perverse people (17:4-5)—their dispersal over the earth is proof of Allah's rejection (7:168). . . . Other sins, some repeated, are enumerated: abuse, even killing of prophets (4:155; 2:91), including Isa [Jesus] (3:55; 4:157), is a consistent theme. The Jews ridiculed Muhammad as Ra'ina (the evil one, in 2:104; 4:46). . . . Precious few of them are believers (also 4:46).[. . .] Jews are blind and deaf to the truth (5:71), and what they have not forgotten they have perverted—they mislead (3:69), confound the truth (3:71), twist tongues (3:79), and cheat Gentiles without remorse (3:75). Muslims are advised not to take the Jews as friends (5:51), and to beware of the inveterate hatred that Jews bear towards them (5:82). The Jews' ultimate sin and punishment are made clear: they are the devil's minions (4:60) cursed by Allah, their faces will be obliterated (4:47), and if they do not accept the true faith of Islam . . . they will be made into apes (2:65/ 7:166), or apes and swine (5:60), and burn in the Hellfires (4:55, 5:29, 98:6, and 58:14-19).

Andrew G. Bostom, "Jihad and Islamic Antisemitism,"
FrontPage Magazine, *May 22, 2008. www.frontpagemag.com.*

said it many times, with an apology to Lord Acton of blessed memory, all utopias kill, and radical, universalistic and apocalyptic utopias kill radically and massively.

We have seen three major ideologies emerging during the 20th century, and in many ways continuing into the present: Soviet Communism, National Socialism and radical Islam. There are vast differences among them, of course, but there also are some parallels. Of interest here, all three ideologies saw or see the Jews as the main enemy, or at least *a* main enemy. We all know about National Socialism. [Joseph] Stalin's Communism saw the Jews as the spearhead of Western imperialism. Radical Islam basically says the same thing: The Jews are the spearhead of Western civilization and they are traditionally the enemies of Islam.

This anti-Jewish ideology has been a part of the development of radical Islam since the late 1920s. The chief ideologue of the movement was the Egyptian Sayid Qutb, an Egyptian official who spent some years in New York and became convinced that the West is decadent and dying.

In 1950 and the years following, he wrote a number of brochures that are the guiding texts of radical Islam to this day. One of them was devoted to the Jews—two years after the establishment of Israel. Traditional Quranic elements intermingled with the legacy of European anti-Semitism, very much influenced by Nazi anti-Semitism. In the Quran, Jews are called apes and swine, because they did not obey their own traditions and their God. They are also branded as the most determined opponents of the spreading Muslim faith, an accusation that is essentially true, because apparently the Jewish tribes of the Arabian desert saw Islam, rightly, as an existential danger to themselves.

Targeting Jews

In the contemporary world, the Jews are seen, as I have already said, as the spearhead of the West. However, they are seen also as more than that—in line with modern European anti-Semitism, Jews are seen as the actual rulers of the West, especially of the United States, through the media controlled by them, and through direct political influence. Thus, Islamistic anti-Semitism sees the fight against the Jews as the first and central piece in their program, and it is preceded, or paralleled, only by their desire to eliminate the present corrupt Arab and Muslim governments, and replace them with Islamic states.

The language used by Muslim media, increasingly under Islamicist influence, is clearly and unmistakably genocidal. Radical Islam wants to annihilate the Jews, contrary to the medieval Islamic principle of seeing them as the People of the Book, who were granted an inferior, but guaranteed, status in Islam. Whether the Holocaust is seen as an inspiration and, if so, whether this is done consciously or unconsciously, I cannot tell. All I can see is that the ideology of Nazism, which led to the Holocaust, is repeated here, albeit in a different dress.

How far is this anti-Semitic ideology influenced by the Israeli-Palestinian conflict? Sayid Qutb wrote his anti-Semitic brochure 17 years before the Israeli occupation of the West Bank and Gaza, so obviously this is not a cause of the rise of this ideology. He wrote it two years after Israel was established, however, and from his point of view the occupation of a piece of land liberated for Islam by its original conquest in the seventh century, and its successful defense against the Crusaders later on, was an outrage and a blasphemy made even more by the fact that the despised Jews accomplished it.

A Genocidal Threat

In 1967, with the occupation of Jerusalem and the rest of the territories, this became the sign of a further terrible defeat that could only be reversed by a total annihilation of the offending people and forces, for theirs was a rebellion against God himself. A compromise reached with the Palestinians, and accepted by them, undoubtedly will reduce the rhetoric and with it the danger, but it will not eliminate it.

This, then, is the major danger that confronts us. We are faced with a genocidal threat to the Jewish people and then to others, as part of another attempt at a universal totalitarian dictatorship, under religious auspices.

What can be done? You cannot defeat an ideology only by force alone. Even in World War II, propaganda on the part of the Allies was a crucial part of the war waged against the Nazis. So the first step must be a mass effort at propaganda to the Muslim world by radio, TV, cassettes, newspapers—and non-radical Muslims must be persuaded to lead that effort.

The second step should be a well thought-out program of economic investments. The Marshall Plan cannot be repeated here, because that was a plan making use of the nascent democratic governments of post-World War II Europe. In the Muslim world, the existing governments must be avoided, because any investment through them would land in the pockets of the ruling. Rather, help should come in the form of pinpointed investments in projects that would develop an infrastructure and encourage local entrepreneurship. These investments should be made through an international agency directly, without being channeled through local governments.

The third step should be a series of formal political alliances throughout the world against radical Islam, involving not only developed countries, but also third-world nations, and especially the non-radical Muslim states of the former Soviet Union.

Finally, force must be used only when it is inevitable, and only when there are concrete targets of direct terrorist activity based on radical Islamist ideology.

A Difficult Movement to Defeat

These are interdependent suggestions and one will probably not work without the others. The guiding thought should be that we are faced with a genocidal ideology that produces genocidal programs and genocidal forces. They are directed toward the Jews, but only initially; ultimately, and quite explicitly, they will be directed against the rest of the non-Islamic world.

One of the characteristics that differentiates radical Islam from Nazism and Communism is the lack of a centralized structure and, [Osama] Bin Laden apart, the absence of a uniting charismatic figure that would combine ideological leadership with political authority. Radical Islamic movements are many and varied—there are at least 17 in Algeria, and a larger number in Kashmir, two in Palestine, and so on. The differences among them are minuscule; they aid and support each other, quarreling over local leadership and tactics, but united in purpose. It is much more difficult to combat a movement like that than it was to face a centralized hostile bureaucracy.

Finally, there is a threatening background to confront. Sayid Qutb was not totally mistaken—the West *is* faced with problems of decadence and regression. The populations of Europe and North America are not growing, or growing only through massive immigration, as in the United States. In the latter case, there may be some reason to assume that the Hispanics coming to the United States will become part of the civilization developed over the past couple of hundreds of years.

The 18 million Muslims who emigrated into Western and Central Europe over the past decades are another story. There are different groups among them, and most of them are not radical Islamists—yet. They do not integrate culturally, however, and the local nationalities are decreasing. In Eastern and Southern Europe, there is a regression of local populations—in Russia and Italy, for example. The number of Jews in the world is static, below the 13 million mark, and is destined to decline markedly in the next half-century.

Radical Islam does have a chance, and world civilization must defend itself against that threat. To repeat—that threat is genocidal. We have been in that scenario before. We must not repeat past mistakes.

Periodical Bibliography

The following articles have been selected to supplement the diverse views presented in this chapter.

Alex Alexiev   "What It Takes," *National Review*, Nov. 7, 2005.

Ramzy Baroud   "We Must Acknowledge Roots of Terror," *The Arab American News*, Aug. 26–Sept. 1, 2006.

Robert Fisk   "Double Standards of Morality: The Age of Terror," *The Arab American News*, Oct. 14–20, 2005.

Reuel Marc Gerecht   "Selling Out Moderate Islam," *The Weekly Standard*, Feb. 20, 2006.

Efraim Karsh   "Islam's Imperial Dreams," *Commentary*, Apr. 2006.

Michael A. Ledeen   "The Advance of Freedom," *Harvard International Review*, Spring 2005.

Shiraz Maher   "How We Can Rid Britain of Violent Extremism," *New Statesman*, July 26, 2007.

Olivier Roy   "Why Do They Hate Us? Not Because of Iraq," *The New York Times*, July 22, 2005.

Shelby Steele   "Life and Death," *The Wall Street Journal*, Aug. 22, 2006.

Brett Stephens   "A Veiled Threat," *The Wall Street Journal*, July 3, 2007.

Mark Steyn   "Jihad, Jihad, Everywhere," *National Review*, Mar. 13, 2006.

Amir Taheri   "Muslim Matryushka," *The Wall Street Journal*, July 7, 2006.

Grif Witte   "Violence: Its Source Is Not Always What It Seems," *Nieman Reports*, Summer 2007.

CHAPTER 2

Does the Qur'an Encourage Islamic Militancy?

Chapter Preface

After the September 11, 2001, terrorist attacks in the United States, blogs and message boards were jammed with posts blaming the attacks on the Qur'an, the Muslim holy book, for encouraging attacks on non-Muslims. For instance, on the *Jihad Watch* Web site, Gregory M. Davis writes in his article, "Islam 101," "The Quran's commandments to Muslims to wage war in the name of Allah against non-Muslims are unmistakable. They are, furthermore, absolutely authoritative as they were revealed late in the Prophet's career and so cancel and replace earlier instructions to act peaceably."

While many commentators categorically reject the notion that the Qur'an actually incites violence, others have pointed out that other holy books also contain passages encouraging violence. In an article in *Reason* magazine, author Cathy Young writes, "The truth is that the canonical texts of every major religion are full of contradictory statements that can be cherry-picked for a variety of messages. The Bible contains expressions of intolerance, from divine commands for conquest and genocide to the mandate of death for anyone who tries to lead a Jew astray from the worship of the one true God."

Dr. Muzammil H. Siddiqi, writing in *Islamic Horizons*, agrees: "Religious texts, if not read within their proper textual and historical contexts, are easily manipulated and distorted." Siddiqi points out a passage from Deuteronomy, the fifth book of the Torah, "I will make my arrows drunk with blood, and my sword shall devour flesh; with the blood of the slain and of the captives, from the long-haired heads of the enemy" (Deut. 32:42).

But Robert Spencer, in *World Net Daily*, responds to these comparisons by saying, "It's true: People of all religions have done terrible things. But none of these kinds of objections gets to the heart of the matter: Terrorists on a global scale today are using the Quran, not the Bible or the Bhagavad Gita or the Book of Mormon, to justify violence."

Certainly, issues of translation and interpretation play a large role in how the Qur'an and other holy books are read, as some of this chapter's authors explain. And, as other chapters in this book explore, many other factors besides the Qur'an must be considered when examining the roots of Islamic militancy.

| "Considered strictly on its own terms, Islam is not a tolerant religion."

The Qur'an Is Inherently Violent and Intolerant

George Cardinal Pell

In the following viewpoint, George Cardinal Pell dismisses claims that Western democracies can coexist with Islam because it is a peaceful religion with varying beliefs, many of which overlap with Christianity and Judaism. Unlike the holy books of these other religions, he says, the Koran is said to be the direct word of God, and therefore, not subject to interpretation. The Koran is filled with incitements to violence and primarily uses "jihad" to mean the waging of war. George Cardinal Pell, the Archbishop of Sydney, Australia, since 2003, is a weekly columnist for Sydney's Sunday Telegraph *and the author of several books.*

As you read, consider the following questions:

1. Which two countries are commonly pointed to as examples of successful Muslim societies, according to Pell?

2. Why does Pell find it unsurprising that much textual analysis of the Koran is carried out by authors using pseudonyms?

3. According to Pell, what conditions are making it easier for Islamic radical groups to gain ground in Pakistan?

Can Islam and the Western democracies live together peacefully? Optimists seize on the assurance of specialists that jihad is primarily a matter of spiritual striving and that the extension of this concept to terrorism is a distortion of koranic teaching. They emphasize Islam's self-description as a "religion of peace." They point to the roots Islam has in common with Judaism and Christianity and the worship the three great monotheistic religions offer to the one true God. There is also the common commitment that Muslims and Christians have to the family and to the defense of life, and the record of co-operation in recent decades between Muslim nations, the Holy See, and countries such as the United States in defending life.

Many commentators draw attention to the diversity of Muslim life—sunni, shi'ite, sufi, and their myriad variations—and the different forms that Muslim devotion can take in places such as Indonesia and the Balkans on the one hand, and Iran and Nigeria on the other. Stress is laid on the widely divergent interpretations of the Koran and shari'a [Islamic religious law], and the capacity Islam has shown throughout its history for developing new interpretations.

Optimists also take heart from the cultural achievements of Islam in the Middle Ages and the accounts of toleration extended to Jewish and Christian subjects of Muslim rule as "people of the Book." Some deny or minimize the importance of Islam as a source of terrorism, or of the problems that more generally afflict Muslim countries, blaming factors such as tribalism and inter-ethnic enmity; the long-term legacy of colonialism and Western domination; the way that oil revenues distort economic development in the rich Muslim states and sustain oligarchic rule; the poverty and political oppression in Muslim countries in Africa; the situation of the Palestinians, and the alleged "problem" of the state of Israel; and the way that globalization has undermined or destroyed traditional life and imposed alien values on Muslims and others.

Reasons for Optimism and Pessimism

Indonesia and Turkey are pointed to as examples of successful Muslim societies, and the success of countries such as Australia and the United States as "melting pots," creating stable and successful societies while absorbing people from different cultures and religions, is often invoked as a reason for trust and confidence in the growing Muslim populations in the West. The phenomenal capacity of modernity to weaken gradually the attachment of individuals to family, religion, and traditional ways of life, and to commodify and assimilate developments that originate in hostility to it, is also relied on to "normalize" Muslims in Western countries.

Reasons for optimism are also sometimes drawn from the totalitarian nature of Islamist ideology, and the brutality and rigidity of Islamist rule, exemplified in Afghanistan under the Taliban. Just as the secular Nazi and Communist totalitarianisms of the twentieth century proved unsustainable because of the enormous toll they exacted on human life and creativity, so too will the religious totalitarianism of radical Islam. This assessment draws on a more general underlying cause for hope: our common humanity. Most ordinary people, both Muslim and non-Muslim, share the desire for peace, stability and prosperity for themselves and their families.

On the pessimistic side of the equation, concern begins with the Koran itself. I started, in a recent reading of the Koran, to note invocations to violence—and abandoned the exercise after fifty or sixty pages, as there are so many of them. In coming to an appreciation of the true meaning of jihad, for example, it is important to bear in mind the difference between the suras [chapters] written during Muhammad's thirteen years in Mecca and those written after he had based himself at Medina. Irenic interpretations of the Koran typically draw heavily on the suras written in Mecca, when Muhammad was without military power and still hoped to win people through preaching and religious activity. After emigrating to Medina, Muhammad formed an alliance with two Yemeni tribes and the spread of Islam through conquest and coercion began. One calculation is that Muhammad engaged in seventy-eight battles, only one of which, the Battle of the Ditch, was defensive. The suras from the Medina period reflect this decisive change.

The Koran's Meaning

The predominant grammatical form in which jihad is used in the Koran carries the sense of fighting or waging war. A different form of the verb in Arabic means "striving" or "struggling," and English translations sometimes use this form as a way of euphemistically rendering the Koran's incitements to war against unbelievers. But in any case, the so-called "verses of the sword" (sura 9:5 and 9:36), coming as they do in what scholars generally believe to be one of the last suras revealed to Muhammad, are taken to abrogate a large number of earlier verses on the subject (over 140, according to one radical website). The suggestion that jihad is primarily a matter of spiritual striving is also contemptuously rejected by some Islamic writers on the subject. One writer warns that "the temptation to reinterpret both text and history to suit 'politically correct' requirements is the first trap to be avoided," before going on to complain that "there are some Muslims today, for instance, who will convert jihad into a holy bath rather than a holy war, as if it is nothing more than an injunction to cleanse yourself from within."

The Christian and Jewish sources of the Koran are an important basis for dialogue and mutual understanding, although there are difficulties. Perhaps foremost among them is the understanding of God. It is true that Christianity, Judaism, and Islam claim Abraham as their father and the God of Abraham as their God. I accept, with reservations, the claim that Jews, Christians, and Muslims worship the same God, but this has been disputed, not only by Christians but by Muslims as well. It is difficult to recognize the God of the New Testament in the God of the Koran, and two very different concepts of the human person have emerged from the Christian and Muslim understandings of God. This has had significant consequences for the different cultures that Christianity and Islam have given rise to, and for the scope of what is possible within them.

Islamic Tolerance Mythical, Not Historic

The history of Muslim relations with Christians and Jews does not offer reasons for optimism in the way that some people easily assume. The claims of Muslim tolerance of Christian and Jewish minorities are largely mythical, as the history of Islamic conquest and domination in the Middle East, the Iberian peninsula, and the Balkans makes abundantly clear. In the territory of modern-day Spain and Portugal, which was ruled by Muslims from 716 and not finally cleared of Muslim rule until the surrender of Granada in 1491, Christians and Jews were tolerated only as dhimmis [non-Muslim subjects of a Muslim State], subject to putative taxation, legal discrimination, and a range of minor and major humiliations. If a dhimmi harmed a Muslim, his entire community would forfeit protection and be freely subject to pillage, enslavement, and murder. Harsh reprisals, including mutilations, deportations and crucifixions, were imposed on Christians who appealed for help to the Christian kings or who were suspected of having converted to Islam opportunistically. Raiding parties were sent out several times every year against the Spanish kingdoms in the north, and also against France and Italy, for loot and slaves. The caliph in Andalusia maintained an army of tens of thousand of Christian slaves from all over Europe, and also kept a harem of captured Christian women. The Jewish community in the Iberian peninsula suffered similar sorts of discriminations and penalties, including restrictions on how they could dress. A pogrom in Granada in 1066 annihilated the Jewish population there and killed over five thousand people.

Arab rule in Spain and Portugal was a disaster for Christians and Jews, as was Turkish rule in the Balkans. The Ottoman conquest of the Balkans commenced in the mid-fifteenth century and was completed over the following two hundred years. Churches were destroyed or converted into mosques, and the Jewish and Christian populations became subject to forcible relocation and slavery. The extension or withdrawal of protection depended entirely on the disposition of the Ottoman ruler of the time. Christians who refused to apostatize were taxed and subject to conscript labor. Where the practice of the faith was not strictly prohibited, it was frustrated—for example, by making the only legal market day Sunday. Violent persecution was a constant threat. One scholar estimates that before the Greek war of independence in 1828, the Ottomans executed eleven patriarchs of Constantinople, nearly one hundred bishops, and several thousand priests, deacons and monks. Lay people were prohibited from practicing certain professions and trades, even sometimes from riding a horse with a saddle, and until the early eighteenth century their adolescent sons lived under the threat of the military enslavement and forced conversion which provided possibly one million janissary soldiers to the Ottomans during their rule. Under Byzantine rule the peninsula enjoyed a high level of economic productivity and cultural development. This was swept away by the Ottoman conquest and replaced with a general and protracted decline in productivity.

No Room for Interpretation

The history of Islam's detrimental impact on economic and cultural development returns us to the nature of Islam itself.

For those of a pessimistic outlook this is probably the most intractable problem in considering Islam and democracy. What is the capacity for theological development within Islam?

In the Muslim understanding, the Koran comes directly from God, unmediated. Muhammad simply wrote down God's eternal and immutable words as they were dictated to him by the Archangel Gabriel. It cannot be changed, and to make the Koran the subject of critical analysis and reflection is either to assert human authority over divine revelation (a blasphemy) or to question its divine character. The Bible, in contrast, is a product of human co-operation with divine inspiration. It arises from the encounter between God and man, an encounter characterized by reciprocity, which in Christianity is underscored by a Trinitarian understanding of God. This gives Christianity a dynamic that not only favors the development of doctrine within strict limits, but also requires both critical analysis and the application of its principles to changed circumstances. It also requires a teaching authority.

Errors of fact, inconsistencies, and anachronisms in the Koran are not unknown to scholars, but it is difficult for Muslims to discuss these matters openly. In 2004 a scholar who writes under the pseudonym Christoph Luxenberg published a book in German setting out detailed evidence that the original language of the Koran was a dialect of Aramaic known as Syriac. Syriac or Syro-Aramaic was the written language of the Near East during Muhammad's time, and Arabic did not assume written form until 150 years after his death. Luxenberg argues that the Koran that has come down to us in Arabic is partially a mistranscription of the original Syriac. He suggests that the Koran has its basis in the texts of the Syriac Christian liturgy, and in particular in the Syriac lectionary, which provides the origin for the Arabic word "koran." As one scholarly review observed, if Luxenberg is correct the writers who transcribed the Koran into Arabic from Syriac a century and a half after Muhammad's death transformed it from a text that was "more or less harmonious with the New Testament and Syriac Christian liturgy and literature to one that [was] distinct, of independent origin." This is a large claim.

Religious Renovation Is Rare

It is not surprising that much textual analysis is carried out pseudonymously. Death threats and violence are frequently directed against Islamic scholars who question the divine origin of the Koran. The call for critical consideration of the Koran, even simply of its seventh-century legislative injunctions, is rejected by hard-line Muslim leaders. Preaching recently [January 9, 2006] to those making the hajj pilgrimage to Mount Arafat, the Grand Mufti of Saudi Arabia told pilgrims that "there is a war against our creed, against our culture under the pretext of fighting terrorism. We should stand firm and united in protecting our religion. Islam's enemies want to empty our religion [of] its content and meaning. But the soldiers of God will be victorious."

Considered strictly on its own terms, Islam is not a tolerant religion, and its capacity for far-reaching renovation is severely limited. To stop at this proposition, however, is to neglect the way these facts are mitigated or exacerbated by the human factor. History has more than its share of surprises. Indonesia has been a successful democracy (with limitations) since its independence after World War II. Islam in Indonesia has been tempered significantly both by indigenous animism, Hinduism, and Buddhism, and also by the influence of sufism. As a consequence, in most of the country, Islam is syncretistic, moderate, and with a strong mystical leaning. This moderate Islam is sustained and fostered in particular by organizations like Nahdatul Ulama, which runs schools across the country, and which, with thirty or forty million members, is one of the largest Muslim organizations in the world.

The situation in Indonesia is quite different from that in Pakistan, the country with one of the largest Muslim popula-

Violence and the Koran

It is self-evident that some Koranic verses encourage violence. Consider for example a verse which implies that fighting is "good for you": "Fighting is prescribed upon you, and you dislike it. But it may happen that you dislike a thing which is good for you, and it may happen that you love a thing which is bad for you. And Allah knows and you know not." (2:216)

On the other hand, it is equally clear that there are peaceful verses as well, including the famous "no compulsion in religion" (2:256).

Resolving apparently contradictory messages presents one of the central interpretative challenges of the Koran. Muslims do not agree today on how best to address this. For this reason alone it could be regarded as unreasonable to claim that any one interpretation of the Koran is the correct one.

Nevertheless, a consensus developed very early in the history of Islam about this problem. This method relies on a theory of stages in the development of Mohammed's prophetic career. It also appeals to a doctrine known as abrogation, which states that verses revealed later can cancel out or qualify verses revealed earlier.

The classical approach to violence in the Koran was neatly summed up in an essay on jihad in the Koran by Sheikh Abdullah bin Muhammad bin Hamid, former chief justice of Saudi Arabia: "So at first 'the fighting' was forbidden, then it was permitted and after that it was made obligatory. . . ."

Mark Durie, "Creed of the Sword," The Australian, *September 23, 2006. www.theaustralian.news.com.*

tions in the world. Of Pakistani Muslims, 75 percent are Sunni, and most of these adhere to the relatively more liberal Hanafi school of Islamic jurisprudence. But religious belief in Pakistan is being radicalized because organizations, very different from Indonesia's Nahdatul Ulama, have stepped in to fill the void in education created by years of neglect by military rulers. Pakistan spends only 1.8 percent of GDP [gross domestic product] on education, and 71 percent of government schools are without electricity, 40 percent are without water, and 15 percent are without a proper building. The population is only 42 percent literate, and this proportion is falling. Such neglect makes it easy for radical Islamic groups with funding from foreign countries to gain ground. There has been a dramatic increase in the number of religious schools (or madrasas) opening in Pakistan, and it is estimated that they are now educating perhaps 800,000 students.

Culture Is Crucial

Indonesia and Pakistan show that there is a range of factors affecting the prospects for a successful Islamic engagement with democracy. Peace and respect for human rights are the most desirable end points, but the development of democracy alone will not suffice. It is not enough to assume that giving people the vote will automatically favor moderation. In its influence on both religion and politics, the culture is crucial.

There are some who resist this conclusion vehemently. In 2002, the Nobel Prize Economist Amartya Sen argued that religion is no more important than any other part or aspect of human endeavor or interest. He also challenged the idea that within culture religious faith typically plays a decisive part in the development of individual self-understanding. Against this, Sen argued for a characteristically secular understanding of the human person, constituted above all else by sovereign choice. Each of us has many interests, convictions, connections, and affiliations, "but none of them has a unique and pre-ordained role in defining [the] person." Rather, "we must insist on the liberty to see ourselves as we would choose to see ourselves, deciding on the relative importance that we would like to attach to our membership in the different groups to which we belong. The central issue, in sum, is freedom."

This does work for some people in the rich, developed Western world, particularly those without strong attachments to religion. Doubtless it has ideological appeal to many more among the elites. But as a basis for engagement with people of profound religious conviction, it is radically deficient. Sen's words demonstrate that the high secularism of our elites is handicapped in comprehending the challenge that Islam poses.

I suspect one example of the secular incomprehension of religion is the blithe encouragement of large scale Islamic migration into Western nations, particularly in Europe. Of course they were invited to meet the need for labor and in some cases to assuage guilt for a colonial past.

Religion, Too, Is Key

If religion rarely influences personal behavior in a significant way then the religious identity of migrants is irrelevant. I suspect that some anti-Christians, for example, the Spanish Socialists, might have seen Muslims as a useful counterweight to Catholicism, another factor to bring religion into public disrepute. Probably too they had been confident that Western forces would be too strong for such a primitive religious viewpoint, which would melt down like much of European Christianity. This could prove to be a spectacular misjudgment.

During the Cold War, secularists, especially those who were repentant Communists, were well equipped to generate and sustain resistance to an anti-religious and totalitarian enemy. In the present challenge it is religious people who are better equipped to understand the situation with Islam. Radicalism has always had a way of filling emptiness, but if we are going to help the moderate forces within Islam defeat the ex-

treme variants, we need to take seriously the personal consequences of religious faith. We also need to understand the
secular sources of emptiness and despair and how to meet
them, so that people will choose life over death. This is another place where religious people have an edge. Western
secularists regularly have trouble understanding religious faith
in their own societies, and are often at sea when it comes to
addressing the meaninglessness that secularism spawns. An
anorexic vision of democracy and the human person is no
match for Islam.

The war against terrorism is only one aspect of the challenge. Perhaps more important is the struggle in the Islamic
world between moderate forces and extremists, especially when
we set this against the enormous demographic shifts likely to
occur across the world, the relative changes in population-size
of the West, the Islamic and Asian worlds and the growth of
Islam in a childless Europe.

Identify Our Friends

Every great nation and religion has shadows and indeed crimes
in their histories. This is certainly true of Catholicism and of
all Christian denominations. And it is legitimate to ask our Islamic partners in dialogue whether they believe that the peaceful suras of the Koran are abrogated by the verses of the sword.
Is the program of military expansion to be resumed when
possible? Do they believe that democratic majorities of Muslims in Europe would impose shari'a law? Can we discuss Islamic history and even the hermeneutical problems around
the origins of the Koran without threats of violence?

Obviously some of these questions about the future cannot be answered, but the issues should be discussed. Useful
dialogue means that participants grapple with the truth and
in this issue of Islam and the West the stakes are too high for
fundamental misunderstandings. Both Muslims and Christians
are helped by accurately identifying what are core and endur-

ing doctrines, by identifying what issues can be discussed together usefully, by identifying those who are genuine friends, seekers after truth and cooperation and separating them from those who only appear to be friends.

> *"No verse in the Qur'an, when placed in its proper textual and historical context, permits fighting others on the basis of their faith, ethnicity or nationality."*

The Qur'an Does Not Condone Or Encourage Terrorism

Islamic Society of North America

In this viewpoint, the Islamic Society of North America (ISNA) asserts its position that terrorism is always unjust, and that the Qur'an condemns it absolutely. "Jihad" is clarified to have several meanings; one of these, combative jihad, is justified only in self-defense under specific conditions, never as vengeance toward non-Muslims. In fact, the authors argue, the Qur'an condemns religious extremism and calls on Muslims to be responsible citizens and co-exist peacefully with people of other faiths. ISNA is an association of Muslim organizations and individuals that aims to provide a common platform for presenting Islam, supporting Muslim communities, and developing educational, social, and outreach programs.

Islamic Society of North America, "Against Terrorism and Religious Extremism," *Islamic Horizons*, vol. 35, no. 3, May/June 2006, pp. 31–32. Reproduced by permission.

As you read, consider the following questions:

1. What are the three contexts in which "jihad" is used in the Qur'an?

2. What criteria must be met before initiating a jihad?

3. According to ISNA, what characteristics of Islam had a major influence on the Renaissance?

Humanity lives today in an interdependent and interconnected world where peaceful and fair interaction, including interfaith and intra-faith dialogue, is imperative. A grave threat to all of us nowadays is the scourge of religious and political extremism that manifests itself in various forms of violence, including terrorism. In the absence of a universally agreed upon definition of terrorism, it may be defined as any act of indiscriminate violence that targets innocent people, whether committed by individuals, groups or states.

As Muslims, we must face up to our responsibility to clarify and advocate a faith-based, righteous and moral position with regard to this problem, especially when terrorist acts are perpetrated in the name of Islam.

Irrespective of the legitimacy of grievances relating to aggression or oppression, *terrorism is the epitome of injustice because it targets innocent people.* Ends do not justify means, and innocent civilians should never pay the price for the misdeeds of others or be used as pawns in settling political or military conflicts. Muslims are bound by the Qur'anic prohibitions of taking an innocent life (Qur'an: 5:32; 17:33), considered as one of the gravest sins in Islam. Furthermore, the Qur'an clearly demands that Muslims act justly and impartially, even when dealing with an enemy (4:135, 5:8).

Jihad is not to be equated with terrorism. Contrary to common misperceptions and mistranslations, the word jihad does not mean "Holy War" or war that is justified by differences in religious convictions. *The Arabic equivalent of "Holy War" is never mentioned in the Qur'an.* There is nothing "holy" about war, and it is described in the Qur'an as a hated act (2:216). The Qur'anic Arabic term jihad and its derivatives mean, literally, *to strive or exert effort*. These terms are used in the Qur'an and Hadith (Prophetic sayings) in three specific contexts: first, in addressing *inward jihad* or the struggle against evil inclinations within oneself (22:77–78; 29:4–7); second in the context of *social jihad*, or striving for truth, justice, goodness and charity (25:52; 49:15); and third, in the *context of the battle-field*, which is often referred to in the Qur'an as Qital (fighting). Combative jihad is allowed in the Qur'an for legitimate self-defense in the face of unprovoked *aggression* or in resisting *severe oppression*, on religious or other grounds (2:190–194; 22:39–41). No verse in the Qur'an, when placed in its proper textual and historical context, permits fighting others on the basis of their faith, ethnicity or nationality.

Conditions for Jihad

Several stringent criteria must be met before combative jihad can be initiated. To begin with, as a "hated act", war should only be undertaken as a last resort after all other means have failed. Next, *jihad cannot be randomly declared by individuals or groups, but rather by a legitimate authority after due consultation*. Finally, the intention of Muslims engaging in combative jihad must be pure, not tainted by *personal or nationalistic agendas*. But even during a wartime situation, the teachings of the Prophet Muhammad (peace be upon him) and of the first caliph, Abu Bakr (r), laid down clear guidelines of behavior on the battlefield. These guidelines forbid the targeting of non-combatants, specifically the elderly, children, women, unarmed civilians and clergy, and the destruction of infrastructure (Sunan Abi Dawood, Bab Al-Jihad; also Tareekh Al-Tabarl).

Whereas war should be undertaken as a last resort to prevent a greater wrong, the ideal and general rule of Muslim behavior is peaceful co-existence with others in kindness and justice (60:8–9). Indeed, the Qur'an *recognizes plurality* in human societies, including religious plurality, as part of God's plan in creation (10:19; 11:118–119). This is why God calls for *peaceful and respectful dialogue*, not forced conversion whether through war or other forms of coercion (2:256; 3:64; 16:125; 29:46).

It is unfortunate that both extremists and detractors of Islam who distort the meaning of jihad propagate a false concept of jihad through expressions such as "jihadists", "Islamic terrorism", or references by terrorists to jihad. Such stereotyping and the use of terms such as "Islamic terrorist" are as unfair as referring to Timothy McVeigh as a "Christian terrorist", or claiming that abortion clinic bombers committed acts of "Christian terrorism". During the course of Muslim history, as has happened with similar norms in other societies and civilizations, the above rules of jihad were violated at different times and in differing degrees. However, the fact remains that *Islamic teachings are to be based neither on the actions of some present or past Muslims, nor on past or present misinterpretations, but rather on the moral principles embodied in Islam's primary authentic sources.*

Tolerance Is Encouraged

Islam does not consider people of other faiths "infidels", and does not advocate violence against them. First, the term "infidel" refers loosely to "someone having no religious faith, an atheist". This word and its meaning are totally incompatible with the Qur'anic statement that the People of the Book (Jews and Christians) believe in the same universal God as Muslims (29:46). Moreover, the term infidel is not a correct translation of the Qur'anic term "Kafir", which means, literally, to cover up or to reject (a belief which is incompatible with one's own). It is used in the Qur'an in various contextual meanings: some are neutral, where farmers are called Kuffar since they cover up the seeds with soil (57:20), some are positive, like re-

The Myth of a Militant Islam

The notion of a militant Islam cannot be supported by any educated reading of the source materials, be they the Qur'an and its commentaries, the *hadith* tradition, or the early Islamic historical works. On the contrary, what is clear when looking at these texts is the remarkable degree of acceptance and, indeed, respect that was shown to non-Muslims, Jews and Christians in particular, at a time—the early medieval period—when tolerance and acceptance of religious differences were hardly well known attitudes. Even in cases of warfare, the Muslim armies acted with remarkable dignity and principle, irrespective of the weakness or strength of their opposition. In short, the early Islamic community was characterized not by militancy, but primarily by moderation and restraint.

These traits were not in spite of the religion of Islam but because of it. This can be seen in the Qur'an in Chapter 2, verse 143, where God says to the Muslims, "We have made you a middle people," that is, a people who avoid extremes, and in another famous verse which says, "... and He [God] has set the Balance [of all things]. Do not transgress the Balance!" (55: 7–8). Traditional Muslims saw all of life in terms of balance.... It has primarily been certain modernized Muslims, whose influences are not the traditional teachings of the faith, but the attitudes and excesses of modernity ... who have transgressed all limits and disregarded the Balance that is true Islam.

David Dakake, Ch. 1,
"The Myth of a Militant Islam," ed. Joseph E.B. Lumbard,
Islam, Fundamentalism, and the Betrayal of Tradition,
Bloomington, IN: World Wisdom, 2004, pp. 28–29.

jecting or disbelieving in idolatry (2:256; 60:4), some refer to the rejection of belief in God, and others refer to rejecting a particular prophet while confessing belief in God.

Second, nowhere does the Qur'an call for violence against anyone merely on the grounds that he/she rejected Islam (2:256; 88:21–22; 6:107–108; 42:48). All verses cited by the users of a "cut-and-paste" approach to claim otherwise (such as 9:5; 29;123), refer to a historical reality when groups or nations from various religious backgrounds engaged in hostilities and aggression against the nascent Muslim community during the Prophet's (p) time. Understanding that historical context and careful textual analysis leave no doubt that the permission to fight back had nothing to do with the religious convictions of these groups or nations, but was due rather to their aggression and gross oppression; it was a state security imperative. *Even if some Muslims have disregarded these clear Qur'anic limits, Islam provides no justification, and cannot be blamed, for such actions.*

Third, it is a disingenuous and misleading tactic to focus exclusively on verses that deal with the contingencies of legitimate self-defense, and to ignore the repeated and consistent statements in the Qur'an that emphasize the *sanctity of human life* (5:32), *respect for human dignity* (17; 70), *acceptance of plurality*, including plurality of religious convictions (5:48 coexistence with all (60:8–9), universal and unbiased justice even with the enemy (4:135; 5:8), *universal human brotherhood* (49:13) and *mercy to all creation* (21:107). The Qur'an is a whole and cohesive book, and should not be interpreted in a piecemeal fashion.

Citizenship and Moderation

Muslims are to act as responsible citizens. It is a well established Islamic principle that citizens of a nation, regardless of its religious makeup, are required not only to uphold the laws of that country, but also to safeguard and protect the security and well being of the country and its people. This principle has recently been reiterated in several statements by the European Council of Ifta' and Research. This Council has called upon Muslim residents and citizens of Western countries to be faithful to the (social) contract according to which they were admitted as residents or naturalized as citizens, since fulfilling one's contracts is a religious duty according to the Qur'an, Hadith and the consensus of Muslim Jurists (see 5:1, 3:76, 17:34 . . .). Acts of terror by citizens of a country are condemnable both because these inflict violence on innocent people, and are treacherous actions that betray the very nature of citizenship.

Islam prohibits religious extremism. Extremism is contrary to the Qur'anic directive to Muslims to be a justly balanced community of believers (*ummatan wasata*) so that, through the example of their lives, they may bear witness to the truth before all humankind (2:143). This verse affirms beyond any doubt that the prescribed course for the Muslim community is the balanced middle way. All extreme tendencies are to be avoided. This injunction towards moderation and balance is emphasized repeatedly in other verses and in the practices and sayings of Prophet Muhammad (p), with reference to areas such as worship, duties to family, marriage, and other affairs. In fact, he specifically warned against extremism and exaggeration in religion (*ghulow*), saying: "Ruined are those who insist on hardship in matters of faith", and instructing his followers to: "Always follow a middle course, whereby you will reach your goal" (Sahih Al-Bukhari). It is these enlightened characteristics of moderation and tolerance, and the inclusion of the contributions of other faith communities and societies that led to the flowering of creativity, knowledge, and invention during several centuries and had a major influence upon the Renaissance.

Peaceful Co-Existence

Muslims are part of the universal human family and are committed to co-existing in peace and justice. Beyond rejecting intolerance and extremism, Islam seeks to bring together people of different races, nationalities and religions, leaving the judgment of theological "correctness" of any person or community to God alone on the Day of Reckoning. While the Qur'an speaks about brotherhood of faith (49:10), it also speaks (in the same chapter) about a broader human family: "O humankind! We (God) have created you from a single (pair) of a male and a female and have made you into nations and tribes, so that you may come to know one another. Verily, the most honored of you in the sight of God is the most righteous (or God-consious) of you. Surely, God is All-Knowing, All-Aware" (49:13; see also 30:22). Note that this verse does not address Muslims exclusively, but rather begins with the inclusive term "O humankind," which embraces all people. It reminds humanity that they belong to one family with the same set of parents, albeit a diverse family, and that their differences are to be celebrated, not causes for division. It is also a reminder that diversity in unity and unity within diversity are possible. This sweeping statement in the Qur'an about a broad human family is a profound basis for peace for and among all people. Beyond stressing the common family roots of all, a basic rule governing the relationship between Muslims and people of other faiths is that of peaceful coexistence, justice and compassion (60:8–9). This verse lays out the duty of Muslims to treat others who are living with them in peace with equity (*gist*) and *birr*. The term birr and its derivatives are the same expressions used in the Qur'an and Hadith to refer to one's relationship with one's parents. Such a relationship is more than kindness, since it also includes love and respect. Building and nurturing this spirit of birr is a cornerstone in the fight against terrorism and religious extremism.

> *"I stand with those who insist that cer-*
> *tain Koranic passages are being politi-*
> *cally manipulated . . . however . . . they*
> *couldn't be exploited if they didn't ex-*
> *ist."*

The Qur'an Can Be Interpreted as Condoning Terrorism, But Does Not Necessarily Do So

Irshad Manji

In the following viewpoint, Irshad Manji challenges the asser-
tions of many Muslims that Islam had nothing to do with the
London terrorist attacks of 2005. She argues that there are, in
fact, passages in the Koran that condone violence, just as there
are such passages in the Bible. Muslims would be better off dis-
cussing their religion honestly and openly, she says. Irshad Manji
is the author of the bestselling book, The Trouble with Islam
Today: A Muslim's Call for Reform in Her Faith, *creator of the*
PBS documentary, Faith without Fear, *and director of the Moral*
Courage Project at New York University.

Irshad Manji, "The 'Sins of Scripture,'" *Maclean's*, August 1, 2005, pp. 18–19. www.macleans.ca. Copyright © 2005 by *Maclean's Magazine*. Reproduced by permission of the author.

As you read, consider the following questions:

1. What factors does the Muslim Council of Britain cite as motives for the London bombings, according to Manji?

2. Why does Manji find these motives to be insufficient to explain the bombings?

3. According to Manji, why do Muslims consider the Koran the immutable word of God, as opposed to other holy books?

It may feel like a case of "here we go again," but the July 21 [2005] bombings in London, combined with the first wave of explosions two weeks before, are changing something for the better. I witnessed that change while in Britain several days ago. As I debated Muslim leaders about our community's response, I nonetheless commended them. Never before had I heard Muslims so sincerely denounce terror committed in our name.

By contrast, the powerless children of Beslan, Russia, didn't have nearly such an effect last year [2004], when armed Islamists stormed their school and starved their bodies over several days. It's as if London—its pluralism, dynamism, and (we shall whisper this) capitalism—marked the line that dare not be crossed.

Then came the kicker. When we all learned that the Muslim suicide bombers were themselves British-raised, the embarrassment felt like a full-fledged exposé. For both reasons, we're finally waking up. Except on one front: the possible role of religion itself in these crimes.

The Muslim Council of Britain insists that Islam has nothing to do with the London bombings. It cites other factors as motives—"segregation" and "alienation," for example. I don't deny that living on the margins can make a vulnerable lad gravitate to radical messages of instant belonging. But it takes more to make him detonate himself and innocent others.

In moments like this, he can't afford the courage of his confusions. He needs conviction. Secular society doesn't compete well on this score. Can one get deathly passionate about tuition subsidies and a summer job? Which is why I don't understand how moderate Muslim leaders can reject, flat-out, that religion may also play a part in these bombings. What makes them so sure that Islam is an innocent bystander?

What makes them sound so sure is literalism. That's the trouble with Islam today. We Muslims, even here in the West, are routinely raised to believe that because the Koran comes after the Torah and the Bible, it's the final and therefore perfect manifesto of God's will. Translation: even moderate Muslims accept, as an article of faith, that the Koran is the untouched, immutable word of God.

This is a supremacy complex. It's also dangerous because it inhibits moderates from asking hard questions about what happens when faith becomes dogma. To avoid the discomfort of questioning our supremacy complex, we sanitize.

The Koran's Potential

And so it was one week after the bombings. A high-profile gathering of clerics and scholars at London's Islamic Cultural Centre produced a statement later echoed by 500 Muslim leaders. It contained this line: "The Koran clearly declares that killing an innocent person [is] tantamount to killing all mankind."

I wish. In fact, the full verse reads, "Whoever kills a human being, except as punishment for murder or other villainy in the land, shall be regarded as having killed all humankind." Militant Muslims easily deploy the clause beginning with "except" to justify their rampages.

It's what Osama bin Laden had in mind when he announced a jihad against America in the late 1990s. Did economic sanctions on Iraq, imposed by the United Nations but demanded by Washington, cause the "murder" of half a mil-

Religious Texts and Violence

[Islam's] scriptures include many passages mandating armed struggle against "unbelievers," ostensibly in response to oppression or persecution of Muslims. Other parts of the Koran, however, explicitly discourage aggression and counsel moderation in the struggle.

The truth is that the canonical texts of every major religion are full of contradictory statements that can be cherry-picked for a variety of messages. The Bible contains expressions of intolerance, from divine commands for conquest and genocide to the mandate of death for anyone who tries to lead a Jew astray from the worship of the one true God. The Gospel of John literally demonizes Jews who do not accept Jesus as children of Satan, and while the gospels promote peaceful evangelizing, Christian doctrine for centuries mandated Christian rule by force.

Cathy Young, "The Jihad Against Muslims,"
Reason, June 2006. www.reason.com.

lion children? Bin Laden believes so (never mind the diversion of aid thanks to an oil-for-food scandal). Did the boot prints of U.S. troops in the Arabian peninsula, birthplace of the Prophet Muhammad, qualify as "villainy in the land"? To bin Laden, you bet. As for American civilians, can they be innocent of either "murder" or "villainy" when their tax money helps Israel buy tanks to raze Palestinian homes? A no-brainer for bin Laden.

And, quite possibly, for the July 7 [2005] terrorists. Right out of the gate, the European jihadist group claiming responsibility cited—what else?—a defence of Iraq and a disgust with the Zionist entity as its primary incentives. The invasion of the former and the existence of the latter amount to nothing less than murder and villainy in the land. Did this interpretation of the Koran guide the British bombers? Because we don't yet know, we can't rule it out.

Muslims Must Be Honest

Yet that's exactly what British Muslim leaders are doing. To be sure, I stand with those who insist that certain Koranic passages are being politically manipulated. Damn right, they are. The point is, however, that they couldn't be exploited if they didn't exist.

We Muslims can't bear to admit as much. Why? Why do we hang onto the mantra that the Koran—and Islam—are pristine? God may very well be perfect, but God transcends a book, a prophet and a belief system. That means we're free to question without fear that the Almighty will feel threatened by our reasoning, speculating, or doubting.

How about joining with the moderates of Judaism and Christianity in confessing some "sins of scripture," as the retired Episcopal bishop John Shelby Spong recently said of the Bible? Muslims would be paying tribute to the very pluralism of ideas and interpretations that allows us to practise our faith in this part of the world.

For now, Muslim leaders are exploiting Islam, not as a sword but as a shield. They're using the sensitivity of religion to protect Muslims from genuine introspection. I don't consider this a favour—to anyone. It's time to lay down the shield and accept the birthright of an open society: that there's no heresy in asking questions. Sometimes pointed questions. Sometimes in public.

Experience tells me that most of my fellow Muslims will reject this principle in the guise of respecting diversity. Which only raises another question: how is it that in diverse societies, those who oppose diversity of thought often feel more comfortable getting vocal than those who embrace it?

> *"One doctrine of Islam dominates in Saudi Arabia—Wahhabism, which is the most extreme, violent, separatist, and expansionistic form of Islam in existence today."*

Islamic Militancy Is Primarily a Product of Saudi Wahhabist Interpretations of the Qur'an

Stephen Schwartz

In the following viewpoint, Stephen Schwartz points out that fifteen of the nineteen perpetrators of the 9/11 terrorist attacks were subjects of Saudi Arabia, a political ally of the United States. He explains that the dominant form of Islam in Saudi Arabia is Wahhabism, the most extreme and separatist form in existence. He argues that this sect not only dominates Saudi Arabia, it also seeks to take over Islam in the West, and it has already made progress in this venture. Stephen Schwartz is a journalist, columnist, and the author of several books, including The Two Faces of Islam: The House of Sa'ud from Tradition to Terror.

Stephen Schwartz, "Radical Islam in America," *USA Today*, vol. 134, no. 2726, November 2005, pp. 16–18. Copyright © 2005 Society for the Advancement of Education. Reproduced by permission.

As you read, consider the following questions:

1. Why did the Muslim community in the United States become much larger in the 1980s and 1990s, according to Schwartz?
2. Which countries did most of these Muslims come from?
3. In Schwartz's view, how have Saudi Wahhabists gained influence on America's prison system?

When the horror of Sept. 11 [2001] first occurred, Americans experienced a great deal of confusion and were subject to much speculation about the motives for such terrorism. It was natural for many of us to assume that we were attacked because of who we are; because we are wealthy, a dominant power in the world, and represent ideas that are in conflict with those of radical Islam. Many also figured—wrongly, I think—that it had mostly to do with the Middle East and Israel. Yet, a very interesting fact emerged—of the 19 suicide terrorists, 15 were subjects of the kingdom of Saudi Arabia.

This is important because these were not poor people from refugee camps on the West Bank or in Gaza, or individuals who had grown up feeling some grievance against Israel and the U.S. because they lived in difficult conditions. These were not people from the crowded and disrupted communities of Egypt or Pakistan, or those who had experienced anti-Islamic violence in the last 20 years and therefore had turned against the U.S. These individuals had grown up in the country that Americans often think of as their most solid and dependable ally in the Arab world.

Why would Saudis be involved in this? What does it mean that Osama bin Laden is a Saudi? Why are so many members of Al-Qaeda Saudis? Why is it that Al-Qaeda essentially is a Saudi political movement? How come 25% of those detained in Guantanamo are Saudis? How is it that a country the U.S. has favored, delivered an enormous amount of wealth to through the purchase of oil, protected militarily, and whose young people have been educated in America for many years is so connected to the attacks of Sept. 11?

Wahhabism in the U.S.

The ideology of Saudi hardliners is, unfortunately for Westerners, of great relevance, even inside the U.S. One doctrine of Islam dominates in Saudi Arabia—Wahhabism, which is the most extreme, violent, separatist, and expansionistic form of Islam in existence today. It not only lashes out at the West, but seeks to take over and impose a rigid conformity on the entire Muslim world.

What then of America? Islam was new in the U.S. in the 1980s and 1990s. Then, because of changes in the immigration laws, the American Muslim community suddenly became much larger. Most Muslims who came here were not Arabs. The plurality have been from Pakistan, India, and Bangladesh. As Islam emerged as a major religion in the U.S., it—unlike other American sects—did not have an establishment. A disparate group of Muslims arrived and established mosques in various places. They represented different ethnic groups and lacked any structure to bring them together and unite them. That situation did not last long, however, because the Saudis decided to create an American Islamic establishment based on the radical doctrines of Wahhabism. In order to bring this about, they created a system of organizations that would speak for American Muslims to the government and the media and through the educational system and the mosques.

One can learn a lot about how the Saudi-backed Wahhabi establishment in the U.S. works by looking at how it came to speak for all of Islam in the American media. It did this by creating a set of organizations. One of the most prominent is called the Council on American-Islamic Relations (CAIR). This group allegedly was set up to be a kind of a Muslim version of the Jewish Anti-Defamation League. That is, its stated goal was to protect Muslims against prejudice and stereotypes.

Influential Muslim Groups

I was working in the newsroom of the *San Francisco Chronicle* at the time, and I was struck by CAIR's approach with our reporters and editors. They did not come to the newspaper offices and say, "We're Muslims; we're here now; this is our holy book; this is the life of our prophet Muhammad; these are the holidays we observe; this is what we believe in and we'd like you to report these things accurately." Rather, they said, "We are a minority and we suffer from discrimination. We suffer from hurtful stereotypes. We know that you are good liberal reporters and that you want to avoid inflicting these stereotypes on us. So, whenever you do a story on Islam, you should call us first and make sure it is correct." Of course, that meant "correct" according to Saudi-sponsored Wahhabism.

There are other such groups. One of them is called the Islamic Society of North America. It is controlled directly from Saudi Arabia, and openly owns 250 of the 1,200 main mosques in the U.S. This, though, is just the tip of the iceberg. My research suggests that a full 80% of American mosques are under the control of the Saudi government and Wahhabism. This does not mean that 80% of American Muslims are supporters of Wahhabism—only that their mosques are controlled by the Saudi Wahhabis. There is a wide range of such organizations. Many we do not hear much about, including some of the worst. For example, the Islamic Circle of North America, which acts as a kind of extremist militia, has a very bad reputation for threatening, intimidating, and enforcing conformity in the Pakistani Muslim community.

Areas of Influence

There are three other areas where the Saudi government and its Wahhabi ideology have gained tremendous influence in the

The History of Wahhabism

Wahhabism is derived from the teachings of Muhammad ibn abd al-Wahhab.... Like most Sunni Islamic fundamentalist movements, the Wahhabis advocated the fusion of state power and religion through the reestablishment of the Caliphate.... What sets Wahhabism apart from other Sunni Islamist movements is its historical obsession with purging Sufis, Shiites, and other Muslims....

In 1744, Ibn Abd al-Wahhab forged an historic alliance with the Al-Saud clan and sanctified its drive to vanquish its rivals. In return, the Al-Saud supported campaigns by Wahhabi zealots to cleanse the land of "unbelievers."...

In return for endorsing the royal family's authority in political, security, and economic spheres after the establishment of the Kingdom of Saudi Arabia in 1932, Wahhabi clerics were granted control over state religious and educational institutions and allowed to enforce their rigid interpretation of *sharia* (Islamic law).

Wahhabism was largely confined to the Arabian peninsula until the 1960s, when the Saudi monarchy gave refuge to radical members of the Muslim Brotherhood fleeing persecution in Nasser's Egypt. A cross-fertilization of sorts occurred between the atavistic but isolated Wahhabi creed of the Saudi religious establishment and the Salafi jihadist teachings of Sayyid Qutb, who denounced secular Arab rulers as unbelievers and legitimate targets of holy war (*jihad*)....

Curtin Winsor, Jr.,
"Saudi Arabia, Wahhabism and the Spread of Sunni Theofascism,"
Mideast Monitor, June/July 2007. www.mideastmonitor.org.

U.S. The first is in the American prison system. With one single exception, all of the Federal and state chaplains representing Islam in this country's prisons are Wahhabis. That is, they are certified by groups originating in Saudi Arabia; the curriculum they follow was created there; and they go into our prisons and preach an extremist doctrine. This is not the same as saying that they go into our prisons and directly recruit terrorists—although there have been cases of that. However, anytime you go into a prison—an environment of violence, obviously populated by troubled people—and preach an extremist doctrine, there are going to be bad and dangerous consequences.

The second area is in the military services. Every single Islamic chaplain in the U.S. military has been certified by Saudi-controlled groups—which means that our military chaplains also hold to Wahhabi doctrines. Is it surprising, then, that we had the incident of the Muslim soldier in Kuwait who attacked his fellow soldiers? Or the problems with military personnel at Guantanamo? Or the Muslim military man in Washington state who was trying to turn over useful information to Al-Qaeda?

Finally, there is the problem with what are known as the Islamic academies: Islamic elementary, middle, and high schools throughout the U.S. are supported by Saudi money and preach the Saudi-Wahhabi doctrine—in some cases to Saudi expatriate children living here but, in many other instances, to Muslim children who are U.S. citizens.

Solving the Problem

This seems a very dark picture. Yet, there are some fairly simple steps to take to solve the problem. First and foremost, it is vital to support the Federal and state governments in a sustained investigation of Islamic extremism in our country. That means not falling for the propaganda claim—made by groups like CAIR—that investigating what is happening in mosques, and the literature being distributed in mosques, somehow violates religious freedom. It is not a violation of religious freedom to prevent extremists from using religion as a cover for sedition and criminality. To the contrary, preventing this is necessary to the defense of religious freedom. So, it is absolutely necessary to support the FBI, Justice Department, and other agencies who are investigating the extent to which Islam in the U.S. is under the influence of anti-American and democratic extremists. Moreover, it is vital that they are empowered to perform these investigations with laws like the Patriot Act.

Second, we must identify and support the moderate and patriotic Muslims in the U.S. who oppose Wahhabism and all it stands for. Many Muslims fit this description, even if we rarely read about or see them. Related to this, we should hold the media accountable for its coverage of these issues. How many times since Sept. 11 has the following accusation been made: "Why is it that more Muslim leaders failed to speak out against this abomination?" Actually, many have done so, but they often have a hard time being heard because their message does not fit the mold that the media likes to impose on this story. Instead, what the media cover are angry Muslims denouncing America's support of Israel and other misleading factors.

Despite all the negatives, there is, of course, many reasons—man's unyielding will to be free among them—to be optimistic about the war on terror around the globe. Yet, let us also not forget, in the course of conducting that war, the importance of stemming the influence of Saudi-supported Wahhabi extremism in our own country.

> *"English translations of the Qur'an have frequently been used to subvert the text as well as its real message."*

Perceptions of Islamic Militancy Stem from Poor Translations of the Qur'an

Ziauddin Sardar

In this viewpoint, British Muslim intellectual Ziauddin Sardar, the author of Desperately Seeking Paradise: Journeys of a Skeptical Muslim, *argues that English translations of the Qur'an generally have aimed to distort its messages. He concedes that it is not an easy text to translate because of its poetic, non-linear structure. Still, according to Sardar, translators have frequently omitted, rearranged, and changed the meanings of passages in the Qur'an, resulting in a more violent and sexist text than the original, subsequently shaping non-Muslim attitudes about Islam. Fortunately, a more accurate English translation of the Qur'an is now available.*

As you read, consider the following questions:

1. According to Sardar, why are translations of the Qur'an not read during Muslims' daily prayers?

Ziauddin Sardar, "Lost in Translation," *New Statesman*, August 9, 2004. www.newstatesman.com. Copyright © 2004 New Statesman, Ltd. Reproduced by permission.

2. How is the Qur'an different from the Torah or the Bible in Sardar's view?

3. What device does the translator Abdel Haleem use to clarify both the subject and context of an address in the Qur'an, according to Sardar?

Translations of the Qur'an have long been a battleground. Ostensibly, the purpose of translating the most sacred text of Islam is to make it accessible to those without Arabic—Muslims and non-Muslims alike. But English translations of the Qur'an have frequently been used to subvert the text as well as its real message. The most obvious point to be made about any translation of the Qur'an (and the correct spelling is Qur'an, not Koran) is that, strictly speaking, it is not the Qur'an. Literally, "*qur'an*" means "reading", or that which should be read. It is an epic poetic text, meant to be read aloud, whose true import can be communicated only in the original. A translation is not that inimitable symphony, the very sounds of which move men and women to tears and ecstasy. It is only an attempt to give the barest suggestion of the meaning of the Qur'an. This is why both classical and contemporary Muslim scholars and jurists agree that translations of the Qur'an cannot be read during daily prayers. Indeed, some scholars go so far as to argue that the Qur'an cannot be written down in letters other than the original Arabic characters. It is not just the heightened language and poetic nature of the Qur'an that creates problems for translators. The Qur'an is not a book like any other. It cannot, for example, be compared with the Torah or the Bible, simply because it is not a book of narrative records of ancient peoples—although it does contain some stories of prophets and earlier nations. It is not a "linear" text with a chronological order or a "logical" beginning, middle and end. Its chapters can be very short or very long. It repeats stories in different chapters, often skips from one subject to another, and offers instruction on the same subject in different places. It has a specific lattice structure that connects every word and every verse with every other word and verse by rhythm, rhyme and meaning.

Botched Translations

European thinkers have frequently used the special structure of the Qur'an to denigrate the Holy Book. The otherwise sensible [Scottish essayist and historian] Thomas Carlyle found the "Koran" to be "a wearisome confused jumble", and declared that only "a sense of duty could carry any European through the Koran". The 18th-century French philosopher and historian Constantin Volney described the Qur'an as "a tissue of vague, contradictory declamations, of ridiculous, dangerous precepts". Given that most European translators have seen the Qur'an in this way, it is not surprising that their translations have left a great deal to be desired. Some have even gone so far as to say that the Qur'an lacks the necessary structure, logic and rationality to be thought of as a book at all.

The first direct translation of the Qur'an into English was by George Sale, in 1734; this, Sale said, provided clear evidence that the Qur'an was the work of several authors. Subsequent translators thought that the only way to make any sense of the Qur'an was to rearrange it into some sort of chronological order. The first translation to do so—by J M Rodwell, rector of St Ethelburga, London—was published in 1861. A more thorough rearrangement was attempted by Richard Bell, a noted Scottish orientalist, whose translation, published in Edinburgh in four editions between 1937 and 1939, was entitled *The Qur'an, Translated, With a Critical Rearrangement of the Surahs.*

Playing havoc with the structure of the Qur'an, however, was not enough. Translators also used omission, distortion and mistranslation to subvert the message and meaning of the Holy Book. Consider, for example, the most widely available translation in English, by N J Dawood, the first edition of which was published by Penguin in 1956. This translation subverts the original in several ways. Often a single word is mistranslated in a verse to give it totally the opposite meaning. In 2:217, for example, we read: "idolatry is worse than carnage". The word translated as "idolatry" is "*fitna*", which actually means persecution or oppression. Dawood's translation conveys an impression that the Qur'an will put up with carnage but not idolatry. In fact, the Qur'an is making persecution and oppression a crime greater than murder. The extract should read: "oppression is more awesome than killing".

At other times, Dawood uses subtle mistranslation to give an undertow of violence to the language of the Qur'an. This is evident even in his translations of chapter titles. "*Az-Zumar*", which simply means "crowd", is translated as "The Hordes"; "*As-Saff*", which means "the ranks", is translated as "Battle Array". "*Al-Alaq*", which literally means "that which clings", and refers to the embryo as it attaches to the wall of the uterus, is translated as "Clots of Blood". Most Muslim translators simply call the chapter "The Clot". What is intended to convey the idea of birth, Dawood projects as the notion of death. Like previous orientalist translators, he also goes out of his way to suggest that the Qur'an is a sexist text. The Qur'an demands that humanity serve God; in Dawood's translation, this injunction applies only to men. Spouses become virgins. Conjuring witches appear from nowhere. Thus, readers of Dawood's version—and most other popular translations of the Qur'an—have come away with the impression that the Holy Book sanctions violence or sexual oppression.

A Faithful and Accessible Reading

For those interested in getting to the heart of the holy text, the good news is that there is now a much more accurate translation available. Muhammad A S Abdel Haleem, professor of Islamic studies at London's School of Oriental and African Studies, has set out not only to translate the text faithfully, but also to make it accessible to ordinary English readers.

Early Translations of the Qur'an

The first translations to English were not undertaken by Muslims but by Christians who sought to debunk Islam and aid in the conversion of Muslims to Christianity. Alexander Ross, chaplain to Charles I (r. 1625–49) and the first to embark on the translation process, subtitled his 1649 work as "newly Englished for the satisfaction for all that desire to look into the Turkish vanities." Interestingly, Ross did not speak Arabic and relied on secondarily translating from the French, a language in which he was not well-schooled.... According to [1734 Qu'ran translator] George Sale (1697–1736), "[Du Ryer's] performance ... is far from being a just translation; there being mistakes in every page, besides frequent transpositions, omissions and additions, faults."

Most eighteenth and nineteenth century translations were undertaken by authors without strong background in Islam.... Among the best known, albeit pejorative, English-language analyses of Islam during this time were those by Christian authors such as George Sale, John Rodwell (1808–1900), Edward Palmer (1840–1882), and Sir William Muir (1819–1905). Of these, Sale was probably the most important because he wrote a detailed critique about earlier translations. His work became the standard reference for all English readers until almost the end of the nineteenth century.... while Sale gave the impression that he based his translation on the Arabic text, others have suggested that he relied on an earlier Latin translation.

Khaleel Mohammed,
"Assessing English Translations of the Qur'an,"
Middle East Quarterly, *Spring 2005. www.meforum.org.*

He achieves this by offering a purely linguistic reading of the Qur'an. He transforms the Holy Book's complex grammar and structure into smooth, contemporary English mercifully free from archaisms, anachronisms and incoherence. The result is both accessible and compelling.

Abdel Haleem makes use of a simple but ingenious device to solve two critical problems. The Qur'an often addresses different parties—for example, the Prophet, or the Community of Believers, or the hostile Meccan tribe of the Quraysh—and switches from one to another in the same verse. Abdel Haleem inserts parentheses to make it clear who is speaking or whom is being addressed. He uses the same device to provide context: for example, when the Qur'an says "those who believed and emigrated", Abdel Haleem adds "[to Medina]". He also includes brief summaries at the beginning of each chapter, as well as judicious footnotes explaining geographical, historical and personal allusions.

Abdel Haleem's emphasis on context—the way that each verse connects with many others, and how the different parts of the Holy Book explain each other—makes this translation a remarkable achievement. For the first time, readers of the Qur'an in translation are able to see that it is a commentary on the life of the Prophet Muhammad. It spans a period of 23 years; and to understand what is going on in any particular verse, you need to appreciate what is happening in the Prophet's life at the moment the verse was revealed. Moreover, to understand what the Qur'an says about a particular subject in one particular verse, you have to know what the Qur'an says about the same topic in different places.

The Limits of Translation

This is why, as Abdel Haleem points out in the introduction, you cannot lift a single verse out of context and use it to argue a point or to show what the Qur'an has to say about something. To illustrate the point, he refers to the oft-quoted verse "Slay them wherever you find them" (2:191). This was taken out of context by Dawood, Haleem argues, and thus used to justify the claim that the Qur'an sanctions violence against non-Muslims; and, after 9/11 [September 11, 2001, terrorist attacks on the United States], to rationalise the actions of extremists. In fact, the only situation in which the Qur'an sanctions violence is in self-defence. This particular verse has a context: the Muslims, performing pilgrimage in the sacred precinct in Mecca, were under attack and did not know whether they were permitted to retaliate. The verse permits them to fight back on this—but not necessarily any other—occasion.

Yet even a translation as good as this has limitations. Despite its originality, it is very much an orthodox reading of the Qur'an. The explanatory footnotes rely heavily on classical commentaries, particularly that of the late 12th-century scholar and theologian Fakhr al-Din al-Razi. And it does not inspire a sense of poetic beauty. But then, in a translation of a text as rich and complex as the Qur'an, you can't expect to have everything.

Periodical Bibliography

The following articles have been selected to supplement the diverse views presented in this chapter.

Tawfik Hamid	"The Trouble with Islam," *The Wall Street Journal*, Apr. 3, 2007.
Nicholas D. Kristof	"Martyrs, Virgins, and Grapes," *The New York Times*, Aug. 4, 2004.
Mark Lilla	"Extremism's Theological Roots," *The New York Times*, Oct. 7, 2001.
Neil MacFarquhar	"Muslim Scholars Increasingly Debate Unholy War," *The New York Times*, Dec. 10, 2004.
Irshad Manji	"Is Islam to Blame? Despite Claims of Moderate Muslims, a Literal Reading of the Koran Offers Cover for Acts of Terrorism," *Los Angeles Times*, July 22, 2005.
Michael Medved	"Admit Terrorism's Islamic Link," *USA Today*, June 24, 2002.
Jonathan Rauch	"A War on Jihadism—Not 'Terror,'" *National Journal*, Apr. 15, 2006.
Salman Rushdie	"The Right Time for an Islamic Reformation," *The Washington Post*, Aug. 7, 2005.
Stephen Schwartz	"Rewriting the Koran," *The Weekly Standard*, Sept. 27, 2004.
David Selbourne	"We Should Learn from Islam's Advance," *The Spectator*, Nov. 4, 2006.
George Weigel	"The War Against Jihadism: Why Can't We Call the Enemy by Its Name? We're Going to Have to in Order to Win," *Newsweek*, Feb. 4, 2008.
Cathy Young	"The Jihad Against Muslims," *Reason*, June 2006.

OPPOSING
VIEWPOINTS®
SERIES

CHAPTER 3

How Should Western Governments Respond to Islamic Militancy?

Chapter Preface

Any attempt to determine how Western governments should respond to Islamic militancy might reasonably begin with an examination of how they have responded in the past. Certainly, understanding past successes and failures is a necessary part of determining future tactics. At the same time, one must bear in mind that assessing the "success" and "failure" of tactics is largely a matter of opinion.

The U.S. government's reaction to the September 11, 2001, terrorist attacks is a case in point. Many international and U.S. commentators have criticized George W. Bush's administration for reacting too strongly—both in terms of domestic policy, including allowing warrantless wiretapping of civilians, and foreign policy, including the decisions to go to war in Iraq and Afghanistan. While other commentators have said that the United States' response was justified, and that the response had to be bold to make up for weak policies that may well have brought on the 9/11 attacks.

In a May 2007 opinion piece in the *Wall Street Journal*, Bernard Lewis wrote that Osama bin Laden has long seen America as a weak nation that could be easily bullied:

> This perception was certainly encouraged and so it seemed confirmed by the American response to a whole series of attacks—on the World Trade Center in New York and on U.S. troops in Mogadishu in 1993, . . . on the U.S.S. Cole in Yemen in 2000—all of which evoked only angry words, sometimes accompanied by the dispatch of expensive missiles to remote and uninhabited places.

Lewis sees this pattern of responses as failing to deter—if not flat-out encouraging—the September 11, 2001, attacks. "The response to 9/11, so completely out of accord with previous American practice, came as a shock," he writes, "and it is noteworthy that there has been no successful attack on American soil since then."

David Selbourne of the British magazine *The Spectator* extends Lewis's assessment beyond the U.S. government. "The West ... is as politically and ideologically weak as the world of Islam is strong," he says. "The West is handicapped by many factors: its over-benign liberalism, the lost moral status of the Christian faith, the vacillations of judiciaries and the incoherence of their judgments, political and military hesitations over strategy and tactics, poor intelligence (in both senses), and the complicities of the 'Left.'" These weaknesses, Selbourne says, "have been skillfully exploited" by Islamic militants.

Writing from the standpoint of a U.S. citizen who has lived through the George W. Bush administration's policies, Maulana Karenga, writing in the *Los Angeles Sentinel*, strongly disagrees with the conclusions of Lewis and Selbourne. Karenga says, "If 9/11 is to have any real and lasting meaning for U.S. society, it requires a sober assessment and rejection of the disastrous policies Bush and company have imposed on this country and the world." Karenga's viewpoint not only focuses more on the negative consequences of the Bush administration policies; it also implicitly rejects Lewis's premise that the United States was attacked because of the way it has responded to attacks in the past.

Still, whether past responses to terrorist attacks are seen as precipitating the 9/11 attacks or not, most political commentators, including those writing in this chapter, agree that the ways Western governments respond to Islamic militancy greatly affects the everyday lives of civilians, as well as many other aspects of governmental policy.

> "And all of this is aided and abetted by the European Union, its liberal immigration laws, its espousal of multiculturalism and, crucially, its implicit disavowal of the concept of a sovereign nation state with a coherent national identity."

Western Governments Have Been Too Tolerant of Islamic Militancy

Rod Liddle

In this viewpoint, Rod Liddle writes that the assassination of Dutch filmmaker Theo van Gogh by Mohammed Bouyeri seems to have awakened the Dutch to the dangers posed by Islamic militants. However, some Dutch still cling to the ideals of tolerance and multiculturalism, even though the denunciations of the murder by the Muslim community are equivocal. Liddle goes on to say that Islamic doctrine of subordination of nationhood to the will of Allah takes advantage of European multiculturalism,

Rod Liddle, "No Tolerance, Please, We're Dutch," *Spectator*, vol. 297, no. 9209, February 5, 2005, pp. 14(2). Copyright © 2005 The Spectator Ltd. UK. Reproduced by permission.

tolerance, and suppression of national sovereignty and identity. Rod Liddle writes the Liddle Britain column. He writes regularly for The Sunday Times *and* Country Life.

As you read, consider the following questions:

1. What does the term "Education by Death" mean, according to Liddle?
2. What was the response of the Muslim community to the murder of Van Gogh, as related by Liddle?
3. What was the response of the Dutch Prime Minister to the murder of Van Gogh, as related by Liddle? Was it effective?

They've been doing a spot of mosque-burning recently, the Dutch. Couple of petrol bombs through the front door and woof—that's Friday prayers postponed indefinitely. I don't suppose they bothered to take their shoes off, either, the perpetrators.

It's all very nasty and very, very unDutch. Holland is the country where everything is allowed, where everything is tolerated, from dope in the coffee houses, to fat-thighed whores baying for your money in frowzy shop windows, to imams suggesting that it's OK to beat up women every now and then. The Dutch model seemed to be this: we'll have our whores and our homosexuals and our cannabis over here and you can smack your women around over there in your Maghrebian ghetto. Live and let live. Mutual tolerance.

But all that is changing. What's happened in Holland is a warning: one commentator calls it 'Education By Death'—the process which made the silent majority in America become militant after 9/11, which galvanised the Australians after the Bali bomb, which led to the fall of the Aznar government after the Madrid train bombing. The transformation of achingly liberal and endlessly tolerant Western people into resolute neocons. And in the case of Holland, the death which has been doing the educating was that of an iconoclastic film-maker and broadcaster, Theo van Gogh, a distant relative of that one-eared painter.

Van Gogh was murdered by a savage from the Dark Ages, a savage with extensive contacts within the world of militant Islam. It was not enough simply to kill him. The assailant, a 26-year-old Dutchman of Moroccan extraction called Mohammed Bouyeri, shot van Gogh eight times. But van Gogh was still not dead, so Bouyeri stabbed him through the heart with one knife and then attempted to hack off his head with another before plunging the knife through his stomach and affixing a scrawled letter of Islamic hatred and illiterate doggerel to the man's body. A letter which also issued a fatwa against a bunch of Dutch politicians, some of whom are now in hiding with the benefit of police protection.

This was back on 2 November. Since then Holland has been in shock. Van Gogh was undoubtedly a controversialist and, despite a background on the unorthodox Left, was not well liked by the liberals. His last film, *Submission*, about Muslim mistreatment of women, was the one that did for him—that and a book called *Allah Knows Best* which showed the author mocked up as an imam. So he was not to everybody's taste. And maybe the Dutch politicians could have been forgiven for expecting his murder—however brutal and horrific and very unDutch—to arouse little more than a passing sadness. But instead, it enraged and frightened the nation—the flowers placed at the site of the murder stretched across the street and around the corner. And then we had the mosque burnings and, by way of retaliation, a few church burnings, too. And, together with this, a fundamental rethink of that old notion, tolerance, and a re-evaluation of multiculturalism.

The West's Pattern of Concessions

The Danish cartoons of the Prophet Muhammad ... have revealed more disturbing things about the West than they have about Muslims in Europe and the Middle East. ...

With Denmark, the initial response of the Bush administration aligned America more with those Muslims who felt the cartoons impugned their sacred messenger than with the European press that had printed the caricatures. Sean McCormack, the assistant secretary of state for public affairs, declared, "Anti-Muslim images are as unacceptable as anti-Semitic images, as anti-Christian images, or any other religious belief." ...

[This response echoes] a common view about Muslim sentiments and Western policy since 9/11. ... To wit: We need to encourage interfaith dialogue, we need to show that the West, particularly America, is not opposed to Islam. ...

However well intended, this empathetic view is seriously wrong-headed. It camouflages what is really at stake in Denmark and the rest of Europe with these cartoons. This type of hearts-and-minds strategy will inevitably backfire, compromising the very Muslims that this administration and liberal Democrats would most like to see advance in the Middle East, Europe, and the United States.

Reuel Marc Gerecht,
"Selling Out Moderate Islam," The Weekly Standard,
Feb. 20, 2006. http://weeklystandard.com.

The Dutch immigration and intervention minister, Rita Verdonk, said this: 'For too long we have said we had a multicultural society and everyone would simply find each other. We were naive.'

Still are, it might be argued. The government has responded to the public clamour by attempting to deport 26,000 illegal immigrants, mostly from Morocco, and introducing a rather more rigorous citizenship test than the one we have in Britain. In Holland, immigrants are responsible for their own integration and must pay 3,000 [euro] to take the test. Failure to comply results in fines or being booted out of the country. Again, all very unDutch. There are other encouraging signs, too: some two thirds of Holland's lower house now wishes to revoke the 1930 Blasphemy Laws (exactly what Labour are now proposing, by the way).

But these are only small stirrings which have done almost nothing to address the fundamental problem—and the anger of the indigenous white population grows more splenetic by the day. I daresay this anger is exacerbated every time a 'moderate' imam appears on television to announce that although he regretted the murder of Thee van Gogh, he's nonetheless very glad indeed that he's dead. This happened just a few weeks ago.

In truth, though, the liberal political elite still clings to this rather fuzzy notion of tolerance, despite the acceptance in government circles that Bouyeri was not a lone nutter but part of an organised Islamic cell known as the Hofstad Group, which constitutes 'a violent movement against the principles and values of the state'. And despite the fact that, as ministers trawl the Muslim ghettoes attempting to make them feel part of a caring and inclusive society, the official Muslim denunciations of the murder are at best equivocal. It's a bit naughty, but we can understand how it happened, they say, shaking their heads. (But not, as it happens, shaking the hands of the female government ministers, because Allah wouldn't like it.)

Shortly after the murder of van Gogh, the Prime Minister, Jan Peter Balkenende, clambered aboard a bandwagon which had been set rolling by a bunch of "concerned" media moppets. This was for everyone in the country to wear an orange wristband signifying unity and tolerance. You can also buy badges bedecked with a picture of a little bumblebee in support of the government slogan 'Bee Tolerant' (geddit?). But it has not done much to pacify the country. Right now, Dutch tolerance is in short supply.

There are broader fears tit large. One recent study suggested that within six years at least three large Dutch cities will have an effective Muslim majority. There's also the nightmare scenario of the Low Countries" caliphate. There are enormous and growing Muslim populations in towns and cities dotted along the coast from Lille to Rotterdam—populations which will one day be in the majority. That'll put an end to the booze cruises, then.

And all of this is aided and abetted by the European Union, its liberal immigration laws, its espousal of multiculturalism and, crucially, its implicit disavowal of the concept of a sovereign nation state with a coherent national identity. Holland is a small country which has become accustomed to not throwing its weight around. It gave tip the guilder without much of a fuss. Its very language seems happy to take a back seat: you will find Dutch far less in evidence at Schiphol airport, for example, than you would find Welsh at Cardiff-Wales airport, and the language of Holland's capital city is, effectively, English.

How, then, do you attempt to inculcate a belief in unity and nationhood among new citizens when the nation is withering away in front of you? For the Islamists, democracy and nationhood are subordinate to the will of Allah, hut for too long Holland has ceded its own democracy and nationhood—and language and currency—to Brussels. Brussels versus Allah. I wonder who would win?

I spoke to one of Theo van Gogh's closest friends, Theodor Holman. He's a columnist and film-maker too. 'We fear the end for the freedom of speech in our country,' he told me. 'Now we are not allowed to say what we believe. We must be very careful. We might be killed. And the politicians who brought us to this mess are not doing anything about it. Orange wristbands!' he laughed. 'Still they tell us we must respect Islam. Why must we?' It is a question you hear more and more frequently; in Holland but also in Britain, where the government pursues the same line of threatening to punish people who attack the Islamic creed while locking up others who espouse it.

Van Gogh was murdered on a cold November morning at 8.40 a.m., just down the road from the huge police station near the Oosterpark. After he had been shot eight times he lay on the ground incapacitated, and Bouyeri approached, gun held out before him. It was during this appalling, terrifying moment that van Gogh, a scourge of the liberals, uttered a very Dutch plea for tolerance.

'Please ... stop ...,' he said. 'We can still talk about this.' And then, as Bouyeri removed his knife: 'Please. Have mercy.'

But he was addressing someone to whom the civilities of Dutch life are anathema. There was no talking to be done. And there was no mercy.

| *"To combat radicalism we must remove grievances, cut away resentment."*

Western Governments Must Address the Grievances That Have Led to Islamic Militancy

John Major

In the following viewpoint, John Major, who served as Prime Minister of the United Kingdom and leader of the British Conservative Party from 1990 until 1997, discusses what must be done to defeat terrorism. He asserts that Western governments must not only fight terrorism militarily, they also must prove the terrorists' messages wrong, by eliminating the grievances terrorists exploit to recruit followers. This includes encouraging democracy and modifying economic policies that leave poor nations behind, as well as promoting peace between Israel and Palestine.

As you read, consider the following questions:

1. What is Al-Qa'eda's main objective, according to Major?

2. Which conflicts have fed the perception that Islam is under attack, in Major's view?

3. What grievance does Major blame Europe and the United States for, in particular?

If the world is to succeed in combating terrorism, then politicians and statesmen must strip away old prejudices and think afresh. That will not always be a comfortable thing to do, for at times it will mean trying to see things from the perspective of the terrorist. I remember how uneasy I felt as prime minister when I spent many hours trying to think myself into the mind of the Provisional IRA [Irish Republican Army]. What I had to do then others must do now—but on a much wider scale.

The fear of global terrorism has replaced the fear of global war. But though terrorism is bolder and more deadly than ever, it has so far failed in its objectives. When Spain, Portugal and Greece dumped fascism, it was not due to terrorism. When communism collapsed in the Soviet Union and Eastern Europe, it was not due to terrorist pressure. [Mahatma] Gandhi was far more successful at effecting change than [Osama] Bin Laden will ever be.

What is the purpose of terror? For many terrorist groups the aim is to radicalise Islam, to set Muslim against non-Muslim, to play upon prejudice, to foster hatred. Al-Qa'eda's objective—a perversion of mainstream, moderate Islam—is the unification of the Islamic community around the world, its purification and the imposition of the most literal translation of strict Sharia law. Bin Laden and his associates wish to see the world divided between Islam and everyone else. Their tactics we know: distortion of the Koran, indiscriminate terror, and the call for a holy war—a jihad—against all who oppose them.

Other terrorists—those in Northern Ireland or Thailand, for example—pursue specific political agendas by unsettling democracies. But always the aim is to create chaos. The economic impact of terrorism is the destabilisation of markets; the political impact is the undermining of civil order and government by consent.

How Democracy Can Win

Terrorism and democracy are polar opposites. As they confront one another, we must ask: is it possible that such a shadowy concept as terrorism can be identified, isolated and defeated? Yes, it can, though we must bear in mind that terrorist groups are rarely entirely destroyed: smaller groups, sometimes made up of the hardest of hardliners, replace them. But, over time, terror can be beaten and the potency of its threat removed.

So, if democracy can win, how can it do so? The answer is complex. One thing we must do right away is rid ourselves of the notion that there is a worldwide terrorist conspiracy. Certainly, some groups have widespread and growing tentacles. Sometimes there is co-operation between several organisations, for some terrorists are mercenaries for hire, unconcerned by any particular cause and motivated only by hatred and greed. But there is no worldwide conspiracy. Most terrorist groups are close-knit, relatively small organisations with their own causes, however perverted, and their own ambitions, however ill-conceived. Their causes may overlap—and occasionally merge—but they are not joined together in one single organisation.

The key here is to recognise that we must take action against existing terror groups today, and implement political measures to prevent the contagion re-emerging tomorrow. To achieve this, all nations threatened by terrorism have a role: a coalition of the willing must embrace every country that wishes to be democratic. These nations must work together to deny terrorists their safe havens, cut off their financing and stem the flow of recruits. They must also, and above all, deny them their causes.

And, to defeat the ideological threat they pose, we must understand the motives that drive them and seek to re-educate those who sympathise with them. We must accept that we cannot win by military power alone, but concede that we cannot win without it.

Eliminate Their Motives

To win, many nations must be engaged in what will be a complex and protracted battle, not least of minds. International co-operation is vital: we need to co-ordinate action against terror, inhibit the movement of terrorists, attack money-laundering, penalise nations that fund terror, reduce their supply of weapons and agree [to] worldwide extradition of terrorist suspects. Yet rendition can only be counter-productive. It is not wise policy.

But these measures alone, though vital policing actions, are not enough to bring victory. We must go further. We must ask ourselves: what motivates terrorism? What encourages non-terrorists tacitly to support them? What can we do to make terrorism so abhorrent as utterly to isolate the terrorist?

The answers to these questions are not always palatable. Radical ideology has fed the perception that the religion of Islam is under attack. Al-Qa'eda asserts this every day. Radicals use this belief as a recruiting sergeant. The Afghanistan and Iraq wars have done much to feed this perception that Islam is under attack. So has the failure to bring the Middle East peace process to a successful conclusion.

The radicals are wrong, but their propaganda is effective. To rebut it, democracies must lessen the chance of demagogues exploiting hardship to promote terrorism. They must fight for the hearts and minds of those into whose ears radical poison is poured. Words alone will not do; they must accept obligations that illustrate the morality of democracy. They must seek to alleviate poverty, disease and injustice.

The wealthy industrial nations must show that we care about the flotsam and jetsam that trail along behind globalisation. We must be concerned at the maldistribution of growing wealth. We must be aware, too, that the free market is bringing about changes that disturb the absolutism of old faiths. We must be aware of the destabilising effects of imposing modern liberalism on ancient tribal cultures.

What the West Can Do

Economic liberalism and radical militancy have grown side by side. Why? One answer is that economic liberalism leaves some people behind—and social and economic marginalisation encourages political radicalisation. The rich nations are not without conscience on these issues but, overall, they do too little. It is thus all too easy to portray the large democracies as uncaring, and every radical voice is keen to recruit converts by doing so.

And the democracies are not entirely blameless. For years, Europe and the United States have been spending broadly seven times as much subsidising cheap food for their own people—who are already well fed—as the whole world spends on all the needs of those whose bellies are swollen with hunger. To combat radicalism we must remove grievances, cut away resentment. By doing so we undercut the message of hate that fuels radicalism.

At the same time we must realise that specific events or conflicts will continue to be used to promote the cause of terror. The Arab-Israeli dispute is one. Palestine has become the issue that is, above all, the poison in the well of relations between Islam and the rest of the world.

The strong support given to Israel is based on admiration for a talented nation forged from a whole history of persecution. Support for Israel does not imply an anti-Palestinian

The U.S.'s War on Terrorism Has Exacerbated Existing Grievances

Before September 11 [2001] and the launching of the "war on terrorism," Osama bin Laden and his band of Islamic revolutionaries appeared to be a spent force with little or no popular support in most Arab societies. However, Bush's "war on terrorism" in general and his war in Iraq in particular have given new life to bin Ladenism by fusing Islamic radicalism with anti-imperial nationalism and by giving Islamic radicalism the foreign imperial enemy it needs to succeed.

The "war on terrorism" thus has created a much larger and more difficult foreign policy challenge. That challenge is not how to militarily eliminate the growing number of local Al Qaeda-inspired terrorist groups but how to damp down the flames of Islamic revolution that US policy has unwittingly helped stoke. . . .

The logical alternative to the Administration's forward-based military offensive would be expanded police, intelligence and special-forces cooperation. . . . This strategy would be combined with an effort to address the legitimate grievances that have led many people in Islamic societies either to support bin Laden's agenda or to hesitate to join the fight against Al Qaeda. Among these are Israel's occupation of Gaza and the West Bank, the stationing of US forces in the Gulf and now the American war in Iraq, which is viewed by many as an attempt to further secure US-Israeli hegemony in the region, including the oil-producing Persian Gulf. . . .

Sherle R. Schwenninger, "A World Neglected,"
The Nation, *Oct. 18, 2004. www.thenation.com.*

bias. And yet, in the eyes of the Muslim world preoccupied with the truly pitiable living conditions in Palestine, support for Israel rankles.

Israel will never be truly safe without acceptance by the Arab states; but Palestine too needs a future. An active peace process is vital for everyone, otherwise there is a vacuum which terror and mayhem will fill. Too often, hope has been dashed for Israelis and Palestinians alike. The continuing dispute has created a playground for the terrorist and, over the years, has so unsettled the political climate in the Middle East that trust has gone and a lasting solution has proved elusive. This plays into the hands of the terrorist, for it gives this dispute a much wider fuse, allowing it to be used to justify terrorism elsewhere.

Facing Reality

At times it is difficult to see how there can be an end to the intransigence, how there can ever be a peaceful solution. It is depressing beyond belief, but it forces us to face the reality: in Palestine, as elsewhere, political progress remains the only way forward. And that progress requires greater understanding of what drives the terrorists; we must, as I stated above, think ourselves into the minds of the gunmen and bombers.

There is much we can learn from experience. We can learn that economic revival is an ally in promoting democracy, and that in lands without hope resentment has a fertile breeding ground. But no one should expect trust to replace suspicion quickly or easily: it is always difficult to wring compromise from entrenched positions. Denouncing terrorists is all very well, and politically safe, but to save lives it may sometimes be necessary to engage with terrorists as well. And, where trust has collapsed, international diplomacy may be needed to supplement national effort. These lessons are eternal.

What else can governments do? A great deal. Islamic governments can speak out about the true nature of Islam, in order to counter the message of the radicals. All governments can work together to encourage inter-faith dialogue. Schools which preach extremism should be pressed to modernise their curricula. Above all, Islamic and other governments can address marginalisation in their societies.

All this—and more—must be part of the anti-terrorist campaign. If we are to repel terrorism and not merely suppress it temporarily, we need to reach out far wider than military and security action alone. Politics and diplomacy must join with policing to capture minds as well as militants. Nothing less will succeed.

"The most common complaint against 'talk' is that it shows weakness, but the truth is that it shows rationality."

Western Governments Should Negotiate with Islamic Militants

John F. Kavanaugh

John F. Kavanaugh is Professor of Philosophy at Saint Louis University, where he also directs the Ethics Across the Curriculum program. In the viewpoint below, he describes the global clashes between the Western and Muslim worlds, and discusses the best methods to solve this crisis. The United States, he says, has already tried the toughness approach, in its war in Iraq. The most effective means of solving this clash of civilizations is for each side to understand the other's point of view and this can only be done through negotiations.

As you read, consider the following questions:

1. Why didn't the war in Iraq work out as the U.S. imagined, according to Kavanaugh?

John F. Kavanaugh, "The Muslim Mystery," *America: The National Catholic Weekly*, vol. 194, no. 10, March 20, 2006, p. 8. www.americamagazine.org. Reproduced with permission of America Press. For subscription information, please call 212-581-4640 or visit www.americanmagazine.org.

2. What is the deepest root of the conflict between the Islamic and non-Islamic worlds, in Kavanaugh's view?

3. According to Kavanaugh, what are the advantages of talking with one's enemies?

Fifteen years ago [1991], one might easily have thought we were entering a new era of peace in the world. The Communist "evil empire" dissolved so quickly, without nukes or invasions, it seemed that swords might indeed be turned into plowshares. An apparently endless cold war ended. Peace dividends danced in our heads. How is it that now we are in such a fix? We face what is presently called an "axis" of evil, made up, primarily and most pressingly, of Muslim states. A few blasphemous cartoons published months ago [September 30, 2005] in Scandinavia triggered riots and protests, after strategic prodding, in a score of countries. France faced its own internal demons in weeks of car burnings throughout its suburbs. An elected leader in Iran spurns the United Nations, aspires to atomic weaponry and calls for the extinction of Israel. Democracy bestows power on a Palestinian terrorist group. Iraq teeters on the edge of a civil war. Bloodletting continues in Africa, often along lines of religion (Christian and Muslim) and race (black and Arab). There is talk of civilizations clashing and European countries having Muslim majorities in three generations.

A choice of such great danger is at hand that the energies of our national discourse must not be wasted on blame. There is enough blame to go around. If one does not think the Muslim world has profound internal problems, one is not serious. If one does not think the West, in particular the United States, has not for over 50 years contributed to our present crisis, one is not being honest. Discussion on these matters of the past will go on. What is more pressing is the path we take for the future.

The two ways that will be presented to us are these: get tough, or get talking. The "toughness" scenario has been behind the invasion of Iraq. Our great show of power would teach the renegade states a lesson. Welcomed as liberators, we next might have moved on Iran. Well, it does not work that way. Terrorists play the "get tough" game as well as anyone, and not with the legal, political and international restraints to which nations generally yield. Since the fall of Communism, certain think tanks have imagined a world dominated by the United States, a world in which no country could challenge or check our power. What might other countries think of such a dream concocted by the most powerful and wealthiest nation on earth, the nation with the most "weapons of mass destruction," the only nation to have used one?

Talking Brings Understanding

I think it is better for us to get talking. Better yet, we might start with some imagination. It is the incapacity of Islamic and non-Islamic worlds alike to imagine the life and thoughts of the other that is the deepest root of our problem.

Imagine yourself a Palestinian Muslim. Your grandfather had a home and vineyard in what is now an occupied territory. It is also non-negotiable that you might ever live in that home again. How do you feel? How do you judge things? How do you look at [Al-Qaeda leader] Osama bin Laden? Is he a fanatic or an ascetic resistance fighter against [President] George W. Bush, who looks to you like an arrogant and superficial apologist for a decadent empire supporting your oppressors? I am not saying our Palestinian is right. I'm just asking you to look at the world as he might look at it.

If you are a Catholic whose father was born in Ireland, you might, like me, have found your earliest allegiances to be with Irishmen and Catholics. My father, a decent and, but for one exception, an unprejudiced man, had one group of people he never trusted. They were the British. He thought the Brit-

How Terrorist Groups End

All terrorist groups eventually end. But how do they end? Answers to this question have enormous implications for counterterrorism efforts. The evidence since 1968 indicates that most groups have ended because (1) they joined the political process or (2) local police and intelligence agencies arrested or killed key members. Military force has rarely been the primary reason for the end of terrorist groups, and few groups within this time frame achieved victory. This has significant implications for dealing with al Qa'ida and suggests fundamentally rethinking post-September 11 U.S. counterterrorism strategy.

Seth G. Jones and Martin C. Libicki,
Summary of How Terrorist Groups End,
Rand Corporation, 2008.

ish were behind most conspiracies and catastrophes in the world. Do you think a Palestinian Muslim might have analogous thoughts?

Then imagine the Gunpowder Plot of four centuries ago. The entire Parliament, as well as the royal family, was targeted for destruction by Catholic subterfuge. Religion and nationalism, once again, were the issues. In our present times, however, Catholics and the Church of England seem to get along.

And that is the point. How did the change come about? For that matter, how did the fall of Communism come about? It was not arms. It was talk. It was information. It was the relationship between a guarded but genial President [Ronald] Reagan and a conscientious [Soviet President] Mikhail Gorbachev.

Grievances Must Be Heard

The most common complaint against "talk" is that it shows weakness, but the truth is that it shows rationality. What is more, it reveals a presumption of rationality in the other party. I am not suggesting that we will find sweet reasonableness in hardened terrorists. Although it has occurred that some former terrorists would later be seen at negotiation tables and even in national leadership, it is quite probable that some Islamic extremists will accept nothing less than the extirpation of all their enemies.

Our relationship to Islam is no impenetrable mystery. The vast majority of Muslims, even those who blame the United States and Israel for all the world's problems (as my father once blamed England) are neither irrational nor evil. They may have just grievances, and they may have distorted views of the West. These grievances and views must be spoken, heard and responded to. Without that alternative, the pull to extremism will only get stronger.

It would be well for us to recognize and publicize the considerable courage of Muslims who have raised their voices against terrorism. From Egypt to Pakistan and on to Indonesia, men and women, often at great risk, have accused the extremists of radical infidelity to Islam. Not to trust the humanity of our Muslim brothers and sisters is ultimately a failure of hope for humanity itself.

*"Engagement is worse than no engage-
ment if it legitimizes Islamist ideology
and alienates non-Islamists."*

Western Governments Should Not Engage Islamist Groups

Zeyno Baran

*Zeyno Baran is a Senior Fellow and Director of the Center for
Eurasian Policy at the Hudson Institute. In this viewpoint, she
discusses an April 2007 meeting between several members of
Congress and members of the Muslim Brotherhood, an Islamist
group. Defenders of this meeting have described the Brotherhood
as a moderate group because it denounces violence. But, Baran
argues, a group should be identified as moderate based on its
ideology, not its tactics. Any group with Islamist ideology is not
moderate. Granting legitimacy to Islamist groups like the Brotherhood endorses this ideology, and fails truly moderate Muslims.*

As you read, consider the following questions:

1. On what belief is the argument for engaging with Islamist groups based, according to Baran?
2. How are non-Islamist Muslims at an organizational dis-
   advantage, in Baran's view?

Zeyno Baran, "O Brotherhood, What Art Thou?" *The Weekly Standard*, vol. 12, no. 30,
April 23, 2007. www.weeklystandard.com. Reproduced by permission.

3. According to Baran, what is the goal of Islamists' "social engineering project"?

Even though Congress was in recess the first week of April [2007], a number of lawmakers kept busy. A bipartisan delegation led by House majority leader Steny Hoyer paid a visit to Cairo, meeting with several Egyptian members of parliament, including members of the Muslim Brotherhood, a controversial Islamist group officially banned in Egypt. Hoyer's contacts with the Brotherhood have added new intensity to the debate over whether or not the U.S. government should "engage" with the group as an ally in the war on terror.

Making the case for such engagement, Robert Leiken and Steven Brooke wrote an article in the March/April [2007] issue of *Foreign Affairs* entitled "The Moderate Muslim Brotherhood." They conclude that the Brotherhood consists of "moderate Muslims with active community support" and that engaging with its members "makes strong strategic sense."

Yet this could not be further from the truth. The argument for a strategy of engagement flows from the incorrect belief that if Islamist groups that denounce violence are strengthened, they will then confront their more violent brethren and rob them of their support base. Although various Islamist groups do quarrel over tactics and often bear considerable animosity towards one another, a "divide and conquer" strategy will only push them closer together. This is illustrated perfectly by the response to Prime Minister Tony Blair's decision to ban the revolutionary Islamist group Hizb ut-Tahrir (HT) after the July 7, 2005, bombings in London. HT reached out to various British Islamist organizations, including the Muslim Brotherhood (despite their intense historical rivalry), and urged them all to stand united or "be the next in line to be proscribed." Sadly, HT's effort was successful and Blair was forced to withdraw his proposal.

Allies in this war cannot be chosen on the basis of their tactics—that is, whether or not they eschew violent methods.

Instead, the deciding factor must be ideology: Is the group Islamist or not? In essence, this means that a nonviolent, British-born Islamist should not be considered an ally. Yet a devout, conservative Muslim immigrant to Europe—one who does not even speak any Western languages but rejects Islamist ideology—could be.

Not a Mainstream Ideology

Moderate, non-Islamist Muslims have long tried to explain the inherent incompatibility of Islamism with a Western society that extols pluralism and equality. Islamists seek the total imposition of Islamic law upon society at large. To the Brotherhood and groups like it, the Koran and Islam are not a source of law but *the only* source of law. As the Muslim Brotherhood declares in its motto, "Allah is our objective, the Prophet is our leader, the Koran is our law, jihad is our way, dying in the way of Allah is our highest hope."

Moreover, engaging with Islamist organizations such as the Brotherhood lends legitimacy to an ideology that does not, in fact, represent the views of the majority of Muslims. Thus, American policymakers who advocate pursuing such a strategy are actually facilitating Islamism by endorsing it as a mainstream ideology. Some have already endorsed organizations that were founded by Brotherhood members and maintain a close ideological affiliation with the group, such as the Council on American-Islamic Relations (CAIR) and the Islamic Society of North America (ISNA). Whether at home or abroad, such a policy is leading to disaster, as liberal, non-Islamist Muslims—having already been denounced by Islamists as apostates—are now being told by Western governments that they do not represent "real" Islam.

Empowering Islamists at the expense of non-Islamists hardly seems a wise strategy for the United States to pursue if it wants to win the war of ideas. After all, non-Islamists are already tremendously disadvantaged in terms of organization

Examination Before Engagement

Many analysts have called on the American administration ... to engage with so-called moderate Islamists in the Arab world. While engagement is necessary, ... the Brotherhood's dangerous political platform should be questioned. Before opening a dialogue with any group—even one that has renounced violence, as the Brotherhood has—there needs to be an examination as to whether a political organization that categorically denies equality on the basis of religion and gender can be lauded as moderate....

Mohamed Elmenshawy,
"The Muslim Brotherhood Shows Its True Colors,"
Christian Science Monitor, *Oct. 12, 2007. www.csmonitor.com.*

and funding. The Muslim Brotherhood has well-established networks of institutions, educational centers, and think tanks, as well as millions of dollars in donations from the Middle East. At the same time, many moderates are deterred from speaking out because of the ire doing so would provoke from Islamist groups. In the West, not only do critics have to worry about *fatwa* calling for their death, but they are also faced with the prospect of getting sued for millions of dollars.

Engagement Is Worse

Indeed, Islamist organizations have flourished in the tolerant environment of the West, taking advantage of the freedom of speech to spread their hate-filled, anti-Semitic ideas without fear of reprisal. In the process, they actively and openly create a fifth column of activists who work to undermine the very systems under which Western societies operate. They are creating self-segregated societies in a process that has been called "voluntary apartheid." This tactic has been enthusiastically supported by the Muslim Brotherhood, whose unofficial spiritual leader Yusuf al-Qaradawi has repeatedly advised European Muslims to create their own "Muslim ghettos" to avoid cultural assimilation.

Islamist groups are engaged in a long-term social engineering project, by which they hope to lead Muslims to reject Western norms of pluralism, individual rights, and the rule of law. At the core of Islamist terrorism is the ideological machinery that works to promote sedition and hatred. That the tactics of the Muslim Brotherhood are nonviolent (or at least *less* violent) does not make the ideology behind those tactics any less antagonistic to the United States.

It may be that, when compared with al Qaeda or Hezbollah, the Muslim Brotherhood is the lesser evil. Yet engagement is worse than no engagement if it legitimizes Islamist ideology and alienates non-Islamists. Recognizing and responding to the threat posed by the Islamist ideology is an important part of the war on terror. Any American or Western engagement with Islamists should be critical in nature. Under no circumstances should we do them the favor of extolling Islamist ideologues as "moderates."

> *"Continuing the fight until a reasonably stable and democratic government holds sway in Iraq is the only way to win the War on Terror."*

Establishing a Pro-Western Democratic Government in Iraq Is Key to Defeating Islamic Militancy

David B. Rivkin Jr.

In the following viewpoint, David B. Rivkin Jr. takes on critics of the Iraq war, arguing that the war in Iraq is an integral part of Islamic militants' battle with the U.S. and allies. Establishing a pro-Western democratic government in Iraq would deny Islamic militants the chance to exploit the popular discontent brought by authoritarian regimes of the past. Conversely, losing the war in Iraq would bolster militant groups in Afghanistan and elsewhere. Rivkin is a partner in the law firm of Baker Hostetler LLP. He served in the Justice Department in both the Ronald Reagan and George H.W. Bush administrations.

David B. Rivkin Jr., "No Substitute for Victory," *National Review*, vol. 58, no. 21, November 20, 2006, pp. 35–38. Copyright © 2006 National Review, Inc., 215 Lexington Avenue, New York, NY 10016. Reproduced by permission.

As you read, consider the following questions:

1. Why does Rivkin disagree with claims that the Iraq war has empowered the Shiites?
2. What was the price of the U.S. retreat from Vietnam, according to Rivkin?
3. In Rivkin's view, why would America's surrender in Iraq strengthen its Islamist enemies, in particular?

Throughout history, countries at war have puzzled and even agonized over how to allocate their scarce military resources. This concern has been particularly acute whenever a nation has confronted multiple enemies spread over a wide geographic expanse, all of whom it could not take on at once. Napoleon, for example, defeated several of the powerful coalitions arrayed against him by engaging their Austrian, Prussian, Russian, and British members in rapid succession. During World War II, President Roosevelt chose a "Europe first" strategy that poured American aid into Britain and Russia at a time when Japan was marching from one success to another in the Pacific theater.

Roosevelt did this even though it was Japan, not Germany, that had attacked the U.S. at Pearl Harbor, and despite strong opposition from the U.S. Navy, much of the American public, and many congressional Republicans reluctant to involve America in a European land war. Roosevelt's decision was driven by the conviction that German military prowess and the possibility of British collapse made the Nazis the most dangerous of the Axis Powers.

It is not surprising, then, that there is a debate now in the U.S. about the proper sequencing of military efforts in the War on Terror. What is surprising—and disturbing—is that, at least with regard to Iraq, the debate is more a slugfest than a serious discussion of the war's underlying strategic questions. The three most important such questions are the connection between the fighting in Iraq and the overarching struggle against Islamist forces worldwide, the impact of possible Iraq outcomes on that broader war, and the prospects for U.S. success in Iraq.

The critics, by and large, maintain that Iraq is not a part of the post-September 11 [2001] campaign against radical Islam. They believe that continuing to fight there would not advance the War on Terror, and would even weaken U.S. ability to prosecute it. Their rationale is that combat in Iraq both misdirects American economic and military resources better spent elsewhere and, per the oft-misquoted recent National Intelligence Estimate, serves as a recruiting poster for jihadists. They also claim that, even if Iraq were lost, the negative strategic consequences would not be serious. By contrast, supporters of our efforts in Iraq hold that the fighting there is an integral part of the war against Islamist terrorism; that, with patience and continued U.S. military investment, a reasonably stable, democratic, and pro-American government can emerge in Iraq; and that the consequences of defeat would be dire.

The Meaning of Mesopotamia

How is one to disentangle these competing claims? When the three strategic questions are considered, the war supporters' answers to at least the first two—the connection between Iraq and the broader War on Terror, and the consequences of American defeat in Iraq—are correct.

To begin with, there is no doubt that, in the minds of our enemies, the fight in Iraq, far from being a strategic distraction, is very much part of fundamentalist Islam's engagement with the United States and its allies. While they wage this war worldwide, they view Mesopotamia as the pivotal theater. To them, expelling U.S. forces from these territories is a necessary prelude to the creation of a global caliphate. This is why the jihadists of the world are pouring into Iraq and dying there by the thousands.

In addition to seeking to inflict a military defeat on the U.S., al-Qaeda and Islamists of all stripes regularly rail against democracy as profoundly anti-Islamic, a mode of governance to be opposed at all costs. Notably, the thinking of both the late Abu Musab al-Zarqawi, a rabid Sunni extremist, and Iran's Mahmoud Ahmadinejad, a rabid Shiite extremist, is deeply hostile to democracy. This is not particularly surprising. The notions of separating the state from religion and letting democratic elections interfere with the divine will are profoundly inconsistent with fundamentalist Islam and its history.

Most critics of the [George W.] Bush administration do not even acknowledge the Islamists' opposition to democracy; or, if they do, they dismiss it as irrelevant rhetoric. But their position is as foolish as that of the Sovietologists who urged Western policymakers during the Cold War to ignore Soviet doctrinal writings. As was the case with the Soviets, the Islamists' words and deeds match perfectly. Indeed, the fact that the insurgency in Iraq has been so fierce, and has drawn so much support from foreign jihadists, demonstrates the Islamists' conviction that Iraq has become the key strategic theater in the War on Terror, and that attempts to build democracy there must be defeated. The efforts of Iran and Syria—America's foremost enemies in the Middle East—to bring about a U.S. defeat in Iraq further underscore the war's importance.

Why Iraq Matters

Iraq matters to the Islamists in a way that, say, Algeria—where they lost a civil war—did not. They do not think it a calamity to be defeated by a secular authoritarian regime, particularly when the U.S. is not directly engaged. Islamist groups have denounced pro-American authoritarian regimes in the Middle East, but not for their democracy deficit. It is, rather, their alliance with the U.S. and their insufficiently Islamic orientation that are anathema to the extremists.

In fact, the extremists find that authoritarian regimes actually aid their strategy. To the extent that such regimes are oppressive and do not provide for the well-being of the populace, the Islamists can ride the wave of popular discontent and channel it to their advantage. Certain Islamist groups may face government repression, as has the Muslim Brotherhood in Egypt and Syria, but secular authoritarianism does not offer a viable ideological challenge to Islamist teachings, especially since pan-Arab nationalism is an utterly spent force. Not surprisingly, secular Arab leaders don lslamist garb whenever it serves their ends. Saddam Hussein, for instance, adopted fundamentalist rhetoric and launched a massive mosque-building program after his defeat in the 1991 Gulf War.

Iraq matters a great deal in the broader War on Terror precisely because building democracy in the heart of the Islamic world enables us to pose an ideological challenge to our enemies—unlike ineffectual soft-sell efforts to convince Islamists of our basic goodness. Similarly mistaken efforts were made during the Cold War, when much of our propaganda was wasted portraying the U.S. as home to a sophisticated society with a vibrant cultural life, impressive athletic attainments, and no feelings of hostility toward Moscow. Students of the Cold War ranging from [American diplomat and historian] George Kennan to [Russian novelist] Aleksandr Solzhenitsyn, while differing in many of their policy prescriptions, correctly maintained that the fight could be won only by combining realpolitik policies challenging Soviet power with a strong ideological attack on Communism. What ultimately captured the hearts and minds of the Soviet people was the demonstration that Communism was spiritually bankrupt, and that democracy was not.

The Impact of Democracy

People in the Middle East likewise do not live by bread alone. It is true that democracy will enhance their quality of life and mitigate their economic and social grievances—a fact oft trumpeted by the Bush administration. But these are not democracy's most important benefits. Far more essential is its ability to vitiate Islamism's spiritual vigor. Indeed, since radical Islam seems to be far better than Soviet Communism at tugging the heartstrings of the dispossessed and even motivating them to commit brutalities, it is even more important now than it was during the Cold War to undermine the enemy's ideological legitimacy.

The Islamist ideology is animated by the idea that sharia-based [Islamic religious law] governance is both inevitable and the only alternative to the Middle East's existing corrupt and authoritarian regimes. Just as the Soviets understood that the demonstration of one Communist regime's illegitimacy would be a demonstration of all Communist regimes' illegitimacy—the real reason for the enunciation of the Brezhnev Doctrine—al-Qaeda and other Islamists readily grasp that the success of democracy in Iraq would have catastrophic consequences for their legitimacy. Indeed, because Iraq's much-maligned constitution fuses Islam and democracy—unlike, say, the secular Turkish constitution—it poses a uniquely powerful challenge to the jihadist ideology. U.S. critics of the Iraqi government focus solely on its shortcomings and fail to realize that the jihadists view its mere survival—no matter how weak it is, or how plagued by internal fighting, or how tenuous its ability to provide security—as a grave threat. The jihadists know that the establishment of a democratic polity that empowers women and calls for all of Iraq's communities to enjoy political and economic rights would be a fundamental blow to their cause. This is the main reason Islamic extremists of all stripes have unleashed horrific violence on Iraq.

The Sunni-Shiite Conflict

What about the argument that U.S. involvement in Iraq was a strategic mistake because it empowered the Shiites? Allegedly, this has helped create a radical Iran-dominated Shiite crescent running from Tehran to Baghdad to Beirut, bolstering the influence of the Islamists in the Middle East. Yet this outcome is neither inevitable nor even likely. Despite common religious affinities, the Shiites are far from united. The two key Iraqi Shiite groups—the Supreme Council for the Islamic Revolution in Iraq and Moqtada al-Sadr's Mahdi Army, which are allied with different factions of the Iranian regime—are divided on the policy issues, including whether to establish a strong Shiite region in southern Iraq and whether to expel the U.S. Indeed, the recent outbreak of fighting among Shiites in southern Iraq highlights the extent of their disunity.

Their divisions in turn dampen the enthusiasm of many Shiite leaders for an all-out confrontation with the numerically weaker but more unified Sunnis. Hence they have a keen interest in the continuation of America's military and political presence in Iraq. Meanwhile, a large portion of the Sunni community is concerned that, notwithstanding all the divisions among the Shiites, it will suffer grievously if the fighting escalates.

Critics have portrayed the intra-Shiite discord and the Shiite-Sunni hostility as insurmountable obstacles to U.S. objectives in Iraq, but they are also strategic opportunities. The U.S. should be able to navigate successfully the shoals of Sunni-Shiite strife and intra-Shiite discord just as we played the Sino-Soviet split to our advantage during the Cold War, and the fighting between the Pashtun-based Taliban and the Tajik-led Northern Alliance during the Afghan War. Over the long term, as Vali Nasr of the Naval Postgraduate School argues in a recent issue of *Foreign Affairs*, the U.S. may be able to build a lasting and positive relationship with the Shiite communities in the Middle East. It may even be possible to use American-allied Shiites in Iraq as leverage against the Shiites in Iran.

Democracy in Iraq Will Have Widespread Results

As Iraqis make progress toward a free society, the effects are being felt beyond Iraq's borders. Before our coalition liberated Iraq, Libya was secretly pursuing nuclear weapons. Today the leader of Libya has given up his chemical and nuclear weapons programs. Across the broader Middle East, people are claiming their freedom. In the last few months, we've witnessed elections in the Palestinian Territories and Lebanon. These elections are inspiring democratic reformers in places like Egypt and Saudi Arabia. Our strategy to defend ourselves and spread freedom is working. The rise of freedom in this vital region will eliminate the conditions that feed radicalism and ideologies of murder, and make our nation safer.

George W. Bush,
Address to the Nation, Fort Bragg, N.C.,
June 28, 2005. www.whitehouse.gov.

To be sure, this kind of bold strategy requires staying power and is incompatible with any of the deadline-driven disengagement plans favored by most of the Democrats. The critics who claim that the Western presence in Iraq inflames the insurgency lose sight of the war's ultimate objectives. Engaging the enemy always creates more hatred and fosters more resistance—right up until the enemy is defeated.

The Specter of Defeat

Given these stakes, even partially successful democracy promotion in the Islamic world and the creation of a modestly pro-American and strongly anti-jihadist government in the heart of the Middle East would be a stunning strategic defeat for al-Qaeda and its allies. It would be a brilliant geopolitical stroke, fusing American idealism with the imperatives of real-politik. Conversely, the consequences of a U.S. loss in Iraq would be manifold and dire. Most obviously, the fates of Baghdad and Kabul are inextricably intertwined. This is because the Taliban and [al-] Qaeda elements in Afghanistan would surely be emboldened by a U.S. defeat in Iraq, while the pro-Karzai forces would be demoralized. A defeat in Iraq would also make it difficult to retain support, both in the U.S. and internationally, for Western efforts in Afghanistan.

More fundamentally, those who claim that the current Hobbesian [referring to the theories of English political philosopher Thomas Hobbes] chaos in Iraq can be neatly separated from other Middle East trouble spots, and that it does not affect America's influence in the region, are utterly wrong. The war of all against all, with nationalism and Islamic extremism thrown in as the major motivating forces, is not limited to Iraq; it occurs frequently throughout the region, appearing in places where American troops have never set foot.

For example, while the Gaza Strip has not seen a level of suicide bombings comparable to Baghdad's, it is rapidly descending into an Iraq-style conflict. Hamas [a Palestinian militant movement combining Palestinian nationalism with Islamic fundamentalism] backers of Prime Minister [Ismail] Haniyeh and Fatah [Palestinian political faction that had led the Palestinian nationalist movement since the 1950s] backers of President [Mahmond] Abbas are battling daily; assassinations of members of these and other Palestinian factions are rampant; and feuds have emerged within both Hamas and Fatah. Regional powers have also become involved, with Iran and Syria backing Hamas and Egypt supporting Fatah. Meanwhile, a new Lebanese civil war—with fighting among the country's Christian, Shiite, and Sunni communities—is a distinct possibility, and religious discord may also emerge in such countries as Jordan and Syria. In this environment, an America that cannot stand the heat in Iraq will be seen as an America that cannot be a credible player elsewhere in the Middle East.

Perceptions of Weakness

We also know that Islamist forces have perceived a long series of American retreats—in places ranging from Vietnam to Beirut to Mogadishu—as a sign that, in [Al-Qaeda leader Osama] bin Laden's charming words, the U.S. is a "weak horse." His sentiment is not uncommon; Islamists are constantly searching for evidence of their foes' weakness. This is apparent in [radical Islamic movement] Hezbollah's intensified militancy following Israel's 2000 pullout from Lebanon; in Shiite claims that Britain's recent withdrawal from Amarah and its adoption of "kinder and gentler" rules of engagement in Basra amount to the beginning of British withdrawal from Iraq, and should be exploited; and in the Taliban's launching of an offensive in Afghanistan when NATO [North Atlantic Treaty Organization]—thought not to have the stomach for a serious fight—assumed greater responsibility there. Perhaps the most telling example of how perceived weakness plays out in the Middle East is the decision of a number of "moderate" Arab intellectuals, in the aftermath of the Israeli military's failure to defeat Hezbollah during the recent fighting in Lebanon, to recant their endorsements of a long-term peace with Israel.

The U.S. retreated from Vietnam after being engaged there politically and militarily for nearly a decade and suffering almost 60,000 war deaths and 150,000 casualties. It paid a huge geopolitical price in the form of emboldened Soviet foreign policy in the 1970s and '80s and a precipitous decline in U.S. credibility worldwide. It would have incurred an even greater cost if not for the collapse of the Soviet Union in the early 1990s. Today, our foes would see U.S. inability to prevail against a determined Islamist insurgency, especially after battling it for a few years and sustaining casualties that are but a small fraction of those we incurred in Vietnam, as definitive evidence of the failure of American will. If the U.S. cannot sustain its war in Iraq, they will reason, it is unlikely to be patient and resilient when confronting future enemies. This conclusion would, to an extent unseen since the years immediately following Vietnam, dramatically diminish the willingness of any government in the Middle East to cooperate with America.

The World Is Watching

Developments in Iraq are being avidly watched around the world, from Tehran to Moscow to Beijing to Pyongyang to Caracas. Given the adaptive nature of warfare, all of our enemies, whether Islamist or not, are certain to use insurgency tactics in any future military confrontation with the U.S., opting for suicide bombings and other means of attacking civilians, possibly in great numbers. Not surprisingly, these tactics have already migrated to Afghanistan. Meanwhile, if America expects difficult and politically unsustainable counterinsurgency campaigns to be a component of future conflicts, its willingness to use force—no matter how great the provocation—will be greatly diminished, and the deterrence value of American military power (including the U.S. nuclear arsenal) accordingly degraded.

This dethroning of American military power would embolden all rogue regimes and terrorist groups. But it would particularly embolden our Islamist foes. Their religious fanaticism would lead them to ascribe an apocalyptic significance to American retreat from Iraq, just as they did to the Soviet defeat in Afghanistan. A U.S. loss in Iraq would be taken as a sign that the time had come to launch ever bolder attacks on American soil and against American interests overseas, and to push for the creation of a global caliphate. Thus, an America that fails to stop suicide bombings on the streets of Baghdad,

Fallujah, and Ramadi is likely to face them on the streets of New York, Washington, and Los Angeles.

The bottom line is that, with our ability to project power against the Islamist forces dramatically diminished, we would have to fight a largely reactive war, focusing mainly on homeland defense against an emboldened enemy. History's lessons concerning such warfare are not encouraging. To take but one example, the Roman Empire in the 4th century ceased strategic offensive operations and, ultimately, was overwhelmed by the barbarians.

Is It Winnable?

These stark realities have become so evident that, in the last several weeks [Fall 2006], even some Democratic critics of the war have begun to concede that U.S. withdrawal from Iraq, no matter how it is dressed up, would be an unmitigated strategic catastrophe. And yet—with astonishing cynicism—they have continued to blast the administration for remaining committed to victory, while claiming that retreat is both inevitable and must be handled as a bipartisan endeavor.

There are, of course, those who claim that the violence in Iraq, and particularly the U.S. failure to stabilize Baghdad over the last several weeks [Fall 2006], demonstrates that military victory is impossible. A recent New York Times editorial made this point with characteristic understatement: "No matter what President Bush says, the question is not whether America can win in Iraq. The only question is whether the United States can extricate itself [without calamitous results]." Yet the notion that the American people, who continued to fight at Valley Forge, Shiloh, Iwo Jima, and Normandy, who persevered and won numerous wars against difficult odds, cannot prevail against the forces of chaos and jihad in Iraq is absurd on its face.

Given the dire consequences of defeat, U.S. policy must be [willing] to do everything possible to prevail. Unless the critics acknowledge this strategic reality, their recommendations concerning the military, political, and diplomatic aspects of U.S. Iraq policy cannot be taken seriously. This does not mean that new military, political, and diplomatic solutions should not be tried. In fact, contrary to the claims of critics who would have us believe that the U.S. has been lurching from one mistake to another, American military operations in Iraq have been remarkably flexible, promptly absorbing lessons learned and constantly innovating.

There are no easy shortcuts to victory. Counterinsurgency campaigns are won by staying in the fight and grinding down the insurgents. Defeating the insurgencies in Malaysia and Algeria took years of hard fighting, with high civilian and military casualties. Convening new diplomatic conferences with Iraq's neighbors, "redeploying" U.S. forces out of Iraq, withdrawing them from combat in major cities, sternly telling the Iraqi government to crack down on Shiite militias, and many other "cures" advanced by critics are in fact placebos. Some of them are positively harmful, such as the notion that we should abandon our pro-democracy efforts and help establish a "strong" government in Baghdad to restore stability. This approach would in fact not make it any easier to provide security, and would vitiate the strategic benefits of building democracy in Iraq. In any case, all of these "solutions" are meant primarily to obfuscate the basic reality of the conflict: We and our Iraqi allies are either going to win by bringing down the level of violence to acceptable levels, with positive political consequences to follow; or we are going to lose. Everything else is window dressing.

Iraq War's Significance Must Be Understood

While further innovations and greater flexibility are needed, the administration's major—and heretofore unfulfilled—task is to convince the American people that the consequences of defeat in Iraq would be disastrous. In a very real sense, the fate of Iraq is determined more in the streets of Washington than in the streets of Baghdad. Americans need to be told again and again that, despite the costs and sacrifices, continuing the fight until a reasonably stable and democratic government holds sway in Iraq is the only way to win the War on Terror. The worst message to send is that victory is impossible and we must now choose between the disastrous and semidisastrous scenarios attendant upon defeat.

Critics who claim that the Iraq War is not of pivotal importance to our existential fight with fundamentalist Islam are dead wrong. While some of them, such as [global financier] George Soros and [media tycoon] Ted Turner, at least honestly acknowledge their mistaken belief that the struggle against radical Islam is not a war at all, the rest deploy warlike rhetoric without understanding what the war is about. To say, as [senator] John Kerry has, that we are really only at war with the group that last attacked us on American soil (al-Qaeda), or to obsess over the fact that Saddam Hussein did not help plan September 11, is to denude the war of its strategic meaning.

[German dictator] Adolf Hitler had nothing to do with the Japanese attack on Pearl Harbor. Japan and Germany were not even coordinating their war strategies against a common enemy, the Soviet Union. Indeed, Japan rather foolishly chose not to engage Russia in the winter of 1941 when the Germans were pressing it hard to do so, and this allowed [Joseph] Stalin to pull Soviet forces from the Far East and rush them to the gates of Moscow. Our World War II foes were animated by different and even inconsistent ideologies. Yet no serious military historian would question that combat with Nazi Germany in the European and African theaters was a part of a broader epochal struggle against the Axis Powers. Likewise, the streets of Baghdad, the dusty roads of the Sunni Triangle, the back alleys of Kabul, and the mountains of Peshawar are all theaters in the global struggle against the Islamists. The surest way to hand them victory is to lose sight of this reality.

| *"Moderate Islam needs to be encouraged internationally."*

Western Governments Should Work with Moderate Muslims to Defeat Islamic Militancy

Robert Spencer

Robert Spencer is Director of Jihad Watch and the author of several books, including two New York Times *bestsellers,* The Truth about Muhammad *and* The Politically Incorrect Guide to Islam. *In the viewpoint below, Spencer asserts that Western governments must encourage truly moderate Muslims while dropping as allies any groups that engage in or support terrorism. In order for moderate Islam to dominate, moderate Muslims must also distinguish themselves from aspects of their religion that encourage Islamic militancy.*

As you read, consider the following questions:

1. On what grounds does Spencer dispute the claim that Islam lays the ground for democratic values?

2. In Spencer's opinion, what do moderate Muslims need to do to ensure that moderate Islam becomes the dominant form of Islam?

3. What risk do moderate Muslims take when they declare their support for the U.S., in Spencer's view?

We do not encourage moderate Islam by pretending Islam is something it isn't or by referring to "Judeo-Christian-Islamic values," as CAIR [Council on American-Islamic Relations], the American Muslim Alliance, and other Islamic advocacy groups in the United States would have us do (actually, would compel us to do, by politically correct coercion).

It serves no purpose to proffer politically correct untruths of the sort uttered by Abdulwahab Alkebsi of the Center for the Study of Islam and Democracy. According to Alkebsi, the essentials of democracy were "consistent with Islam's clarion call for justice, equality, and human dignity. . . . According to the Qur'an, one of the explicit purposes of God's messengers is to offer mankind liberty, justice, and equality." Islam, he said, "lays the ground for the values of freedom, justice, and equality that are essential to democracy, more so than any other religion or dogma."

If this is so, why didn't the Islamic world ever give rise to a democracy until the establishment of secular Turkey, which was heavily influenced by the West—where ideals like democracy, freedom, justice, and equality run from the classical Greeks, through the Christian era, through today? Alkebsi also doesn't make clear whether the Qur'an's offer of freedom, justice, and equality to mankind extends to all regardless of creed, or is conditional upon conversion to Islam. Whether they were intentionally deceptive or simply a massive exercise in wishful thinking, Alkebsi's words on behalf of moderate Islam ring hollow not only for informed non-Muslims, but, more importantly, for radical Muslims as well.

Muslims Must Take the Initiative

Ultimately, if moderate Islam is ever to become the dominant form of Islam around the world, the impetus must come from Muslims themselves. They must do it by explicitly renouncing some aspects of Islamic tradition and history—most especially jihad and dhimmitude—and by combating them when they appear as terrorism. Many are taking this initiative. But what the West means by terrorism is not always synonymous with what Muslims mean by it. The Saudi-based Muslim World League said in May 2003 that "terrorism was the most dangerous challenge facing Muslim countries and called for a broadly-based front to eradicate it." The league's secretary general, Sheikh Abdullah al-Turki, lamented that "the events of September 11 [2001] have aroused some fear and mistrust between people in the Muslim World and the West." Of Muslim radicals he said, "It is unfair to take such individuals as representatives of Islam and Muslims."

Yet al-Turki's Muslim World League (MWL) continues to spread Wahhabi Islam, with its insistence on traditional faith and practice (including, presumably, traditional teachings on jihad and dhimmitude) around the globe. On March 20, 2002, federal agents raided the MWL offices in Virginia on the suspicion that the league had ties to terrorist groups. They had good reason to think they might find something there. Mohammad Jafal Khalifa, [Al-Qaeda leader] Osama bin Laden's brother-in-law, "through his foundation, has allegedly been supplying arms and other logistics to Abu Sayyaf bandits" in the Philippines, "some of whom also claim to have been trained in bin Laden's terrorist camps in Afghanistan." Khalifa's "foundation" is the International Islamic Relief Organization (IIRO), the self-described "social arm" of the Muslim World League.

What Makes a Group Moderate?

In considering [Muslim] groups, it is possible to set out some basic criteria by which to judge whether they are indeed parties with whom America might pursue a constructive relationship.... As we see it, there are six questions to be asked of any such group.

- Does it both espouse democracy and practice democracy within its own structures?

- Does it eschew violence in pursuit of its goals?

- Does it condemn terrorism?

- Does it advocate equal rights for minorities?

- Does it advocate equal rights for women?

- Does it accept a pluralism of interpretations within Islam?

Any group that meets these six criteria seems to us to merit support and cooperation, and groups that go a long way toward meeting them deserve at least a second look. To be sure, it would be a grievous error to chase after Islamists at the expense of the secular liberals who are our most natural allies.... But just as we once found friends and allies among those who had come through the Communist mill, so we may also find friends and allies ... among moderate Islamists or those who have come through the Islamist mill.

Joshua Muravchik and Charlie Szrom,
"In Search of Moderate Muslims,"
American Enterprise Institute Website,
February 1, 2008. www.aei.org.

A Heated Battle

Such endeavors are fraught with other perils as well. If moderates are perceived as tools of the United States, they risk losing all credibility among their own people—particularly the radicals whose minds they have to change. In declaring his support for jihad against American forces in Iraq, Sheikh Muhammad Abu Al-Hunud of the Palestinian Authority referred to American protests against material in Saudi textbooks and issued a warning against moderate or "Americanized" Islam. "The aggression against Iraq is an assault on Islam, the Koran and the message of Muhammad. . . . If, God forbid, something happens to Iraq, the aggression and the Crusade will turn tomorrow against the Koran. Prior to the attack on Iraq, Allah's enemy and the enemy of His Prophet . . . called to change the religious education systems in the Arab and Islamic countries. Today, God forbid, his second assault is on the Koran, [he wants] to change verses and to mess with Allah's book, to Americanize the region, Americanize the religion, Americanize the Koran, Americanize Muhammad's message."

There is an increasingly heated battle for the soul of Islam. "What matters now," says Hasan al-Banna's [Egyptian Islamic reformer and founder of the Muslim Brotherhood] grandson Tariq Ramadan, "is that Muslims abandon their fear that self-criticism plays into the hands of the West." Some Muslims and ex-Muslims are ready to engage in that criticism in order ultimately to bring health and true peace to Islamic society. According to Iranian philosopher Dariush Shayegan, "We have sanctified the Sharia. But the Sharia is very cumbersome in the Islamic world! It keeps society from moving. This kind of Islam, it is sclerotic Islam, petrified! The time has come for us to break the taboos." Boualem Sansal, an Algerian writer, calls for a new interpretation of Muslim sources—*ijtihad*. "For lack of ijtihad," he says, "Islam is out of step with the times. It crushes more than it elevates; it controls more than it liberates." He said that Muslim countries were "led by bloody charlatans," aided in their oppression by the Qur'an, which "lends itself to all bad interpretations." He noted that "contempt for women" is buttressed by "hundreds of verses."

Concludes [secularist author] Ibn Warraq, "It is time for moderate Muslims to question honestly the principles of their faith. To admit the role of the Qur'an in the propagation of violence. For them to see this text for what it is: a human text, containing serious moral, historic, and scientific errors."

Encourage Moderate Islam

Moderate Islam needs to be encouraged internationally. The Tunisian writer Al-'Afif Al-Akhdar recently attacked in print Muslims who "generate terror through religious Jihad education—an education which all Arab countries implement, except Tunisia." May other countries follow Tunisia's example.

One way America can help is by reconfiguring its alliances with the Muslim world. Any state that prefers the Sharia to friendship with the United States should be dropped as an ally. Painful as this might be in the short term, to do otherwise is self-defeating, as America has presumably learned in Saudi Arabia; moreover, it is one very tangible way to encourage moderation in the Islamic world.

> "... engagement with such people is the current strategy, and the result is that radicalisation of Britain's Muslims is going through the roof." ...

Western Governments Working With Moderate Muslims Will Not Defeat Islamic Militancy

Melanie Phillips

In this viewpoint, Melanie Phillips, British columnist and author, discusses a speech given by Communities Secretary Hazel Blears on how the British government should counter Muslim extremism. Phillips praises Blears for making the point that it is not enough to counter terrorism, but it is necessary to counter extremist ideas, such as the desire to impose a Muslim Calliphate over all societies. However, Phillips criticizes Blears for suggesting that the British government engage with the "moderate majority" of the Muslim community, while in the course of her speech giving the impression that this "moderate majority" actually holds extremiest views. Phillips, in the course of her dicussion, suggests that there are "truly moderate Muslims" but that

Melanie Phillips, "A Less Than Engaging Strategy," *The Spectator*, February 27, 2009, pp. 1–4. Copyright © 2009 The Spectator Ltd. Reproduced by permission of *The Spectator*.

*no person who believes in the imposition of sharia law and sup-
ports the enemies of one' country or terrorism in other parts of
the world can fit into that category. Engaging with these kinds of
moderates, who do not commit violence themselves but who support the violence of others, emboldens them, rather than pacifies
them. Melanie Phillips writes articles, mainly about social and
political issues, for the* Daily Mail *newspaper and maintains a
blog hosted by* The Spectator.

As you read, consider the following questions:

1. What are the names of some of the groups who hold
   extremist views, according to Phillips?
2. Why is it difficult to engage or negotiate with those who
   hold extremist views, according to Phillips and Blears?
3. How is it possible to identify "true" moderates, according to Phillips?

A couple of weeks ago, there were claims on Panorama and
in the *Guardian* that the government was about to make
a drastic change to its strategy for tackling Muslim extremism
in Britain. According to these claims, it realised it had made a
catastrophic error in identifying extremism with violence, thus
ignoring the conveyor-belt of extreme Islamist ideas which is
radicalising ever rising numbers of young British Muslims—
and, worse still, engaging people with those extremist ideas as
government advisers on combating Islamist violence. At the
time, I expressed scepticism about such an outbreak of real-
ism and suggested it was more likely that an argument was
going on in Whitehall between these two factions.

On Wednesday evening, the Communities Secretary Hazel
Blears delivered a major speech on the subject which, far from
presaging a change in strategy, was a defence of the status
quo. But it was so incoherent and nodded simultaneously at
so many competing arguments that it seems even more likely
that, just a few weeks before the government is set to an-

nounce the second phase of its counter-extremism strategy, the argument behind the scenes about the direction it should take is indeed still raging.

The essence of the muddle in this speech was her blurring of the distinction between moderate and extremist Muslims, and between tackling only violent extremism (as at present) and tackling extremist ideas. At one point early on in the speech she seemed to well understand the key point that until now the security world has denied—that it is not enough to tackle terrorism, because extremist ideas by people who are not themselves violent nevertheless act as a continuum of prejudice, hatred, sedition and violence:

> But the question is the extent to which politically-extreme groups such as Hizb ut-Tahrir contribute to an environment which makes violence more acceptable or justifiable, makes individuals more susceptible to committing acts of violence, and whether there is a symbiotic relationship between groups whose hate is expressed in words, or whose support for terrorism or suicide bombing is confined to the Middle East but not Britain, and those whose hate is expressed in violent actions. For example the Muslim Brotherhood is not a terrorist organisation, but it supports terrorist organisations such as Hamas in Gaza.

Indeed. And so did that mean that the government would now treat the Muslim Brotherhood as beyond the pale and stop throwing money at them and employing them as government advisers in the wholly misguided belief that they were the antidote to terror? Well no. Because although the common threads in this network of violence and hatred were

> a belief in the supremacy of the Muslim people, in a divine duty to bring the world under the control of hegemonic Islam, in the establishment of a theocratic Caliphate, and in the undemocratic imposition of theocratic law on whole so-

cieties: these are the defining and common characteristics of
the disparate strands of this ideology here and around the
world,

nevertheless this was all a

twisted reading of Islam

which was not shared by the vast majority of British Muslims who

oppose the single narrative promulgated by Al-Qaeda, and
certainly oppose violence.

But she had just gone to some lengths to explain that the
problem was not just al Qaeda but also people who did *not*
support violence but the political Islamisms whose extremist
ideas helped promote that violence. So what was she going to
do about *them* the political Islamists—was what we now
needed to know.

But she didn't tell us. Instead, she retreated to the old
comfort zone of the 'moderate majority' and the need to engage with and encourage the mainstream Muslim community
so that violence would not take further root there. And then
her speech started skidding all over the road:

You can see the potential dangers inherent in this approach.
Every minister is well aware of them. It involves engaging
with organisations and individuals with whose views we disagree vehemently, who, for example, have unacceptable attitudes towards women, Jews, or gay and lesbian people. As a
Government anchored in the European social democratic
tradition, we place great store in equality, women's rights,
anti-racism, and so on.

So there is a need for moral clarity, for a clear dividing line
between what we consider acceptable, and what we consider
beyond the pale.

We are clear that engagement is not the same as endorsement. I know our political opponents will seek to make hay

U.S. Aid Can Undermine Middle East Democracy Activists

Efforts by Western governments and nongovernmental organizations (NGOs) to bolster local human rights networks and reform-minded organizations are backfiring from Egypt to Malaysia as moderate dissidents see their credibility with local populations rapidly erode or, even worse, find themselves the objects of government persecution. . . .

Perhaps the most obvious example of a political crackdown in a Muslim nation designed to combat Western-led democratization efforts is the case of Iran. The U.S. State Department announced in February 2006 an earmark of $75 million for a "democracy fund" to promote civil society in Iran.

Moderate-leaning political activists in the nation . . . quickly warned the plan would end in disaster. Fatemeh Haghighatjoo, an Iranian reformist politician, said in a conference at The Carter Center in May 2006 that such open financial support from the United States automatically put NGOs in danger.

*Source: "How U.S. Aid Can Undermine
Middle East Democracy Activists,"
The Carter Center Website, August 23, 2007
http://www.cartercenter.org*

with this: they will say that somehow engaging with groups with extremist views shows a lack of proper understanding of them, that we're being hoodwinked, used, or exploited by extremists, or that we don't care enough about anti-Semitism, sexism or homophobia. This is at the core of the argument of, for example, Melanie Phillips.

But if we leave the field clear to extremists, without any engagement at all, we embolden them and undermine our own objectives. And if we genuinely want to change minds, then we will never make progress merely by talking to people who already agree with us. We must be prepared to challenge, and be challenged in return.

But now she appeared to be saying that the mainstream Muslim communities with whom the government was having all this dialogue actually had extremist views. So while earlier she had been talking about the importance of engaging with moderates, now she seemed to be talking about the importance of engaging with extremists. And as she said, I do indeed think that such 'engagement' is 'endorsement'; more importantly, truly moderate Muslims think so too and have repeatedly begged the government not to engage with extremists in the community because it emboldens them and undermines true moderates .

Blears went on:

What is needed is a framework for engagement, based on clear principles.

Indeed: and those principles should surely be that it is not just support for violence in Britain that should be beyond the pale but advocacy of a caliphate, a desire to overturn British society and impose sharia law, or support the enemies of this country or terrorism abroad. But no, the minister declared merely that she would not sit down with advocates of terrorism because:

You cannot win political arguments with groups who tell lies as part of their strategy, who change the goal-posts, who spread misinformation and seek to undermine the very process of debate. Agreeing to meet and engage in discussion with such groups would lend a veneer of legitimacy that they have done nothing to warrant.

But it is not just terror groups who fit this description but political Islamists such as the Muslim Brothers. Yet with groups which display

> an equivocal attitude on core values such as democracy, freedom of speech or respect towards women,

there would be 'limited engagement'. Did that include the Muslim Brothers, or Hizb ut Tahrir, or other groups who want to Islamise Britain? Because engagement with such people is the current strategy, and the result is that radicalisation of Britain's Muslims is going through the roof while the government is seen to cave into the threat of violence and dance to their tune. Witness, for example, the banning of the Dutch anti-Islamist politician Geert Wilders, who threatens no-one, while according to the Centre for Social Cohesion the Hezbollah spokesman Dr Ibrahim el-Moussaoui is to be allowed into the country to teach a course on political Islam at the School of Oriental and African studies—*a course apparently aimed at educating Government officials and the police.*

So lets get this straight—'engagement' with extremists means having a spokesman for an Iranian terrorist organisation responsible for numerous attacks upon western interests 'teach' British officials and police officers about the inspiration for that terror.

It defies belief. No wonder there's an argument going on in Whitehall.

| "The British reaction to the assault on their capital has provided lessons in civil society and liberty to which America's leaders should pay attention."

The U.S. Government Should Follow the Example of the British Government and Respond to Islamic Militancy with Respect for Civil Liberties

Samuel Loewenberg

In this viewpoint, Samuel Loewenberg, a staff writer for the political Web site Politico, *compares the British and American governments' reactions to the July 7, 2005, transit system bombings in London and the September 11, 2001, attacks on New York City and Washington, D.C. Britain's government, he says, immediately and clearly distinguished those responsible for the attacks from Islam itself. It also put into place mechanisms to fight terrorism without unnecessary infringements on the civil liberties of its citizens. The U.S. government, Loewenberg argues, should take its cue from the British government when it comes to responding to terrorism.*

As you read, consider the following questions:

1. According to Loewenberg, how did the U.S. government react to the September 11, 2001, terrorist attacks?
2. What are the main differences between the terrorist attacks in the United States and Great Britain that Loewenberg mentions?
3. How is London's Muslim community different from those of other Western cities, according to Loewenberg?

Finished with their Sunday morning of studying the Koran, the dozens of young boys in the Muslim Center in east London raced to put their shoes back on. Talking excitedly, they filed upstairs to spend the rest of the afternoon playing Arabic board games and Ping-Pong. Three days earlier [on July 7, 2005] terrorist bombs had ripped open three subway cars and a double-decker bus, taking the lives of at least 52 people and injuring 700. Now, life was getting back to normal.

The Muslim Center, which adjoins a mosque, is just a 10-minute walk from where one of the bombs went off. And for the city's 600,000 Muslims, the bombings had made their place in society suddenly precarious. Some Islamic organizations had issued warnings for Muslims to stay off the streets for fear of reprisals.

But by the weekend, the streets were again bustling with veiled women and men wearing traditional beards. "Yes, I'm worried, but I'm not overly worried," says Shibbir Ahmed, a local government official who volunteers with the Young Muslims Organization U.K. Ahmed, who was born in Bangladesh but grew up in England, said he has faith in Londoners' ability to maintain respect for different cultures. The terrorists, he said, "are trying to destroy that social cohesion. But I don't think they will succeed."

American Versus British Reaction

So far it seems that Britain will not go the way that America did after September 11 [, 2001]. Following the World Trade Center and Pentagon attacks, while anti-Muslim attacks were relatively scarce, there was a general hysteria about terrorists "in our midst." The government, if anything, was more hysterical than the citizenry, with legislation that ran roughshod over civil liberties, as well as mass arrests and eventually the detention of more than 13,000 people. There were mass arrests, deportations, public displays of military might, and clash-of-civilizations media coverage, like *Newsweek*'s cover story "Why They Hate Us," which bore a picture of a turbaned child holding a machine gun.

Of course, there are big differences between the 9-11 attacks and the London transit bombings, not least because of the (thankfully) much-smaller death toll. Britons were not caught unawares, having long expected an assault on their capital. It's also something for which they have decades of experience, from the Nazi blitz during World War II to more recent Provisional IRA [Irish Republican Army] bombs.

Yet even with the different scale and historical context, the British reaction to the assault on their capital has provided lessons in civil society and liberty to which America's leaders should pay attention. Within a day of the attacks, Londoners were back on the Underground and in pubs. They could do this because their institutions, political parties, police, and media had all withstood the attacks as well.

An Atmosphere of Mutual Respect

There have been some scattered anti-Muslim incidents, especially in the North where Muslims are a small minority but a substantial one in many towns. About a half-dozen mosques suffered assaults, from graffiti to arson, and at least one Muslim man was assaulted. But Islamic leaders attribute these actions to extremists or thugs, and say that overall, they continue to be well treated by British society. In particular, they praised the restraint shown by politicians, the police, and the media in the aftermath of the attacks.

"They have all been extremely responsible," said Massoud Shadjareh, the chairman of the Islamic Human Rights Commission, an advocacy organization in London. "I am surprised myself that I am saying so, speaking as someone [who] is usually critical of their actions," he said.

In a press conference after the attacks, Metropolitan Police Deputy Assistant Commissioner Brian Paddick made a special point of disassociating Islam and terrorism. "The words 'Islam' and 'terrorist' do not go together," he said. "These acts go totally against what I understand is the Muslim faith."

Anwar Ali, an 18-year-old who works in an Islamic bookshop around the corner from the Muslim Center, said that while he wasn't surprised to hear of anti-Muslim incidents in economically troubled northern England, where there has been longtime friction, he did not expect serious trouble in London, with its cosmopolitan spirit. "There's mutual respect," Ali says. "Everyone's all right with each other."

Britain's Unique Context

London's Islamic community occupies a unique place in the Western world. It is the most diverse in terms of class, country of origin, and history. It makes up fully 8 percent of the city's population. People of South Asian descent appear as newscasters and soap-opera characters, sports stars and business leaders, yet at the same time, many Muslims maintain traditional dress, with women in veils and men in traditional clothing seen in both rich and poor neighborhoods. "There is a lot more confidence in Britain to hold on to your identity and be part of your society," says Shadjareh.

The British reaction also stands in contrast to that of the Spaniards, who, after the Madrid attacks of March 11, 2004, reacted with massive public demonstrations, denouncing both

Rating of Bush Administration—Fighting Terrorism, Protecting Civil Liberties

"How would you rate that the Bush administration has done fighting terrorism?"
"How would you rate that the Bush administration has done protecting civil liberties?"

Base: All Adults

	Fighting Terrorism		Political Party		Protecting Civil Liberties		Political Party	
	Total	Rep.	Dem.	Ind.	Total	Rep.	Dem.	Ind.
	%	%	%	%	%	%	%	%
Positive (NET)	**38**	**73**	**14**	**32**	**33**	**65**	**12**	**28**
Excellent	12	31	2	7	7	19	2	3
Pretty good	25	42	12	25	26	45	11	25
Negative (NET)	**59**	**24**	**84**	**66**	**57**	**28**	**80**	**65**
Only fair	30	18	39	33	22	21	24	25
Poor	29	6	45	32	35	7	56	41
Not sure	4	3	2	3	9	8	8	7

Note: Percentages may not add up exactly to 100% due to rounding.

TAKEN FROM: The Harris Poll #132, "Bush Administration Gets Low Marks on Balancing Fighting Terrorism and Protecting Civil Liberties," Table 1, December 28, 2007. http://harrisinteractive.com.

the war in Iraq and what they saw as a cover-up by the conservative party then in power, which resulted in that government's ouster. Here, though, party politics has remained at the sidelines.

In the United States, the post–9-11 response was most apparent in subway stations and shopping malls, where commuters and shoppers suddenly found themselves being watched over by machine gun-wielding National Guardsmen. This GI Joe response was ostensibly to protect against further attacks, although how a potential machine-gun battle in the middle of Grand Central Station was supposed to make anybody feel at ease is unclear. It did, however, mentally prepare Americans for the feeling that they were at war—and appropriately so, one supposes, considering that they were about to embark on two.

Protecting Civil Liberties

Britain already has an official secrets act that allows prior censorship, a domestic intelligence agency, the MI-5, and a very extensive network of video-camera surveillance. But it also has had a potent civil-liberties backlash in response to police excesses during the years of the Irish Republican Army bombings. A British law allowing indefinite preventive detention for suspected terrorists, enacted in December 2001, was overturned last December [2004] by the Law Lords, Britain's counterpart to the U.S. Supreme Court. Current law allows house arrest in some circumstances, but only with the personal approval of the home secretary. The [Tony] Blair government is seeking new anti-terrorism legislation, but it is being resisted by rank-and-file MPs [Members of Parliament] in all three major parties, including Blair's own.

"We are very conscious of the fact that we don't want to tear up our civil liberties," says Ramesh Chhabra, the spokesman for Tory Party Shadow Home Secretary David Davis. Chhabra said that while the Conservative Party has long complained about the current immigration system, it's not going to use the attacks as a way to promote tightening the law. And in comparison with the religious rancor that erupted in the United States, with Christian leaders like Franklin Graham referring to Islam as "a very evil and wicked religion," England's Islamic, Christian, and Jewish leaders issued a joint statement condemning the attacks.

"The interreligious community is strongly united, but it is in a state of fragility after acts like this," said the Reverend Alan Green, the Church of England representative who has been meeting with Muslim leaders, since the July 7 attacks. "We have been as proactive as possible to show that the different faith communities stand together."

Londoners, so far, are following the lead of Mayor Ken Livingstone, who said, "We won't let a small group of terrorists change the way we live."

Periodical Bibliography

The following articles have been selected to supplement the diverse views presented in this chapter.

Martin Bright	"The Task Force Was a Sham," *New Statesman*, July 3, 2006.
Mathias Doepfner	"Europe, Thy Name Is Cowardice," *The American Enterprise*, Oct.–Dec. 2005.
The Economist	"Britain: The Wake-Up Call that Wasn't: One Year on," July 8, 2006.
Francis Fukuyama and Adam Garfinkle	"A Better Idea," *The Wall Street Journal*, Mar. 27, 2006.
F. Gregory Gause III	"Can Democracy Stop Terrorism?" *Foreign Affairs*, Sept./Oct. 2005.
Mark Helprin	"They Are All So Wrong," *The Wall Street Journal*, Sept. 9, 2005.
Llewellyn D. Howell	"Solving the Middle East," *USA Today*, Sept. 1, 2006.
Michael Rubin	"All Talk and No Strategy: The Limits of Diplomacy," *Weekly Standard*, July 24, 2006.
Andrew Stephen	"My Fellow American Muslims . . . ," *New Statesman*, July 9, 2007.
Bruce Stokes	"Next Steps on Terrorism? No Consensus," *National Journal*, Sept. 10, 2005.
R. James Woolsey and Nina Shea	"What About Muslim Moderates?" *The Wall Street Journal*, July 20, 2007.
Fareed Zakaria	"How We Can Prevail," *Newsweek*, July 28, 2005.
Waleed Ziad	"Jihad's Fresh Face," *The New York Times*, Sept. 16, 2005.

OPPOSING
VIEWPOINTS®
SERIES

CHAPTER 4

How Should Citizens Respond to Islamic Militancy?

Chapter Preface

Much of the Western media's discussion of how Muslim citizens should respond to acts of terrorism committed in the name of Islam, is based on a premise that these citizens typically do not condemn such attacks. But this very premise is debatable and, indeed, debated. A look at the Muslim reaction to the September 11, 2001, attacks provides a microcosm of the debate over the Muslim response to Islamic militancy.

On October 3, 2001, former British Prime Minister Margaret Thatcher voiced a frequently heard criticism of the Muslim response to September 11: "The people who brought down those towers were Muslims and Muslims must stand up and say that is not the way of Islam. They must say that it is disgraceful. I have not heard enough condemnation from Muslim priests," she said.

Many such criticisms were exacerbated by reports and videos of Palestinians celebrating the attacks in the West Bank town of Nablus. According to a Fox News report, "About 3,000 people poured into the streets of Nablus shortly after the attacks began, chanting 'God is Great' and, in their traditional gesture of celebration, handed out candy."

While such incidents undoubtedly took place, it is also clear that many Muslim leaders, organizations, and individuals issued clear messages that denounced the September 11 attacks. The political leaders of Pakistan, Libya, Syria, Iran, and Egypt all issued statements condemning the attacks. A September 27, 2001, fatwa, an Islamic religious ruling, condemning the attacks was issued by a group of Islamic scholars from Egypt, Syria, and Qatar. A letter to *The Guardian* was sent by nine British Muslim leaders saying, "Such indiscriminate acts of terror are an affront to humanity at large. Islam condemns such abhorrent behaviour and the Holy Koran equates the murder of one innocent person with the murder of the whole of humanity." As the BBC reported, "In Iran, vast crowds turned out on the streets and held candlelit vigils for the victims. And at a Tehran's football stadium, 60,000 spectators respected a minute's silence."

If Muslims have condemned the attacks in great numbers, why have Americans and their sympathizers not heard them? Paul M. Barrett, author of the book, *American Islam: The Struggle for the Soul of a Religion*, writes in a 2007 *Salon* article, "Muslim Americans who attend my readings often [tell me], sometimes with great emotion, that they have repeatedly denounced terrorism but that non-Muslims don't listen." Barrett hypothesizes that this apparent lack of communication "may also have to do with the way American Muslims have condemned terrorism. Specifically, until recently, Muslim leaders often added caveats to their condemnations that robbed them of real force." For instance, while many Muslim leaders strongly criticize the acts carried out by the September 11 terrorists, they sometimes agree, at least to some extent, with their criticisms of the U.S. policies in the Middle East.

The Muslim response to the July 7, 2005, London transit system bombings reveals that the Muslim community may have learned something since 2001, Barrett surmises. Groups such as the Council on American-Islamic Relations (CAIR) and the Islamic Society of North America (ISNA) renounced the London attacks with a "new bluntness" that he believes is both "laudable and welcome." While some of the authors included in this chapter disagree with Barrett, all have opinions about how citizens should respond to Islamic militancy.

> *"The real 'war on terrorism' can only be won if the religious, political and intellectual leaders of Islamic countries and communities actively confront and fight . . . Islamist extremism."*

Islamic Militancy Can Be Defeated Only by Muslims, Not by Western Governments

Anthony H. Cordesman

In the following viewpoint, Anthony H. Cordesman asserts that Islamic militancy is primarily an ideological and regional threat, rather than a global political or economic threat. As such, he argues, it can only be defeated by Muslim citizens themselves at the local religious level, rather than by Western governments, whose efforts have historically been self-defeating. Cordesman holds the Arleigh A. Burke Chair in Strategy at the Center for Strategic & International Studies (CSIS). He is a national security analyst for ABC News and former National Security Assistant to Senator John McCain.

Anthony H. Cordesman, "Winning the 'War on Terrorism': A Fundamentally Different Strategy," *Middle East Policy*, vol. 13, no. 3, Fall 2006, pp. 101–108. www.mepc.org. Reproduced by permission of Blackwell Publishers.

As you read, consider the following questions:

1. According to Cordesman, why are Western efforts to democratize the Middle East more self-defeating than using military force in that region?

2. Why does Cordesman recommend that counterterrorism efforts have a national, rather than regional, focus?

3. Why is the "long war" a dangerous term, according to Cordesman?

The latest events [2006 civil war] in Somalia are yet another warning that the United States, its Western allies and Islamic nations need to change their strategies to win the "war on terrorism." The basic lessons have been the same in Iraq, Afghanistan and throughout the Islamic world. The present mix of Western action and Islamic inaction cannot possibly win.

Part of the problem is conceptual. The United States and most Western nations may be "politically correct" when they call the current struggle a "long war" or "global war on terrorism," but the reality is very different. Most terrorism is a minor and largely national threat. The real threat is Islamic extremism, specifically neo-Salafi Sunni Islamist extremism. The violent transnational movements that support these beliefs, symbolized by al-Qaeda, are the only serious global threat that uses terrorism. Isolated terrorist movements do need to be defeated, but Irish, Spanish, secular Palestinian, Sri Lankan, Japanese and other such groups are peripheral threats at most.

Recognizing this fact, and focusing on it, is critical to any hope of winning the real "war on terrorism." The struggle is religious and ideological, not military or driven by secular values. It is a struggle for the future of Islam, and it is not generic, global or focused on political or economic systems.

As such, the real war on terrorism can only be won within Islam and at a religious and ideological level. This does not mean that improving every aspect of counterterrorism at the national, regional and global level is not important. It does mean that no amount of outside action by the United States, Europe or non-Islamic states can do more than partially contain the violence. It is only the religious, political and intellectual leaders of Islamic countries and communities, particularly in the Arab world, that can successfully engage and defeat Islamic extremism at a religious, intellectual, political and cultural level.

Limits of Western Military Intervention

The West does need to actively protect itself against terrorism and try to deny movements like al-Qaeda sanctuaries in such places as Afghanistan, Iraq and Somalia. Whether or not anyone likes the word "war," Islamist extremist violence is so dangerous that it must be met with force. The current efforts to transform U.S. and other Western forces in order to give them better area and language skills and true expertise in counterinsurgency and counterterrorism are also vital.

The West needs to understand, however, that none of these measures will ever enable the West to "win." They at best enable Western forces to score limited tactical victories, help local forces contain major terrorist movements, defend home territory and buy time. If the West seeks to use major long-term deployments of U.S., British or other non-Islamic forces to fight sustained struggles in Islamic countries, the end result will be to breed new extremists and terrorists. As Afghanistan and Iraq have shown, military and counterterrorist battles need to be won by local and Islamic forces, not "occupiers," "crusaders" and "neo-imperialists."

There are too many memories of colonialism, and there is too much anger against U.S. ties to Israel, for Western forces to succeed unless they act in alliance with local forces and local governments that are clearly sovereign. Moreover, even the United States will never be able to deploy the number of needed troops or have enough forces with necessary language skills and area expertise. It will always have to rotate too much of its force too quickly to build up the personal relationships critical to success.

Islamist extremists have already shown how well they can exploit any long-term presence of "outside" forces. But Western efforts to train and equip effective local forces have a very different effect. They can create enough local forces to do the job, and such forces will start with all the necessary area and language skills and personal relationships, and be able to stay on the scene. Moreover, Western military, counterterrorism, counterinsurgency, and intelligence training and advisory efforts can introduce methods and tactics that show proper respect for human rights and the rule of law in those cases where such reform is necessary. . . .

Political Reform: Evolutionary Change

More generally, the United States and its Western allies need to understand that the wrong kinds of efforts to "reform" the Middle East can lose the war on terrorism at precisely the ideological, political, cultural and religious levels where it must be won. Like it or not, the short- and mid-term battles against Islamist extremism and the day-to-day action in counterterrorism are going to have to be won or lost by existing regimes. Creating open-ended political instability and its consequent broad popular hostility cannot win a religious and ideological struggle fought out by those with a different culture and faith.

Western efforts to push instant political change and "democracy" are more dangerously self-defeating than Western efforts to use military force. As Algeria, Iraq, Kuwait, the Palestinians and Saudi Arabia have shown, elections do not mean progress unless there are national political movements that advocate practical courses of action. Electing Islamists and/or provoking civil war do not bring political stability and cannot defeat a religious and ideological movement. "Democracy" can only make things better if it is built on sound political and legal checks and balances that protect minorities and prevent demagogues and extremists from coming to power. Elections do more harm than good if they divide a nation in ways that encourage violence and civil conflict.

As Iraq has shown all too clearly, the long history of sectarian violence and tribal wars has not been erased from the minds of much of the Middle East. Western efforts to achieve instant democracy can easily provoke a crisis in traditional societies. Where parties do not now exist, rushing to create them will result in entities that are sectarian, ethnic or tribal in character. Where they do exist, the better-organized and disciplined parties will come to power. In most cases, such parties have an Islamist nature: Hamas, Egyptian Islamic Jihad and the Islamist parties in Kuwait.

Local Versus Outside Reform

Efforts by "occupiers," "crusaders" and "neo-imperialists" to impose change from the outside, rather than encourage it from within, cannot succeed. In fact, neo-Salafi Islamist extremists often do a fine job of using such efforts to discredit internal reform efforts and reformers. Furthermore, the West needs to accept the fact that an evolutionary approach to change means working with many local leaders who are not democratic, fall short of Western ideals or are "traditional" in character. Calls for regime change and other efforts that introduce political instability and produce more resistance to reform will do far more harm than good.

Political reform must be built on a foundation of moderate political parties, a real rule of law, and a respect for human rights that protects all but the most extreme voices in a society. Developing a true culture of political participation will take a decade or more. Most of the impetus for political reform also must come from within and be led by local political leaders and reformers.

It is equally impractical to call for rapid economic, social and demographic reform to remove the causes of terrorism. In practice, such calls to "drain the swamp" and eliminate popular support for extremism are at best a well-meant fantasy. The demographics of virtually all Arab and Islamic states have already created a youth explosion of new students and entrants to the labor force that will be a major problem for the next two decades.

Economies, societies and birth rates do not change quickly. They can only change in ways that bring internal stability if change is in response to internal political and social dynamics that move at a measured pace. As is the case with political reform, the West can do a great deal over time by working with moderate political leaders and local reformers, by focusing on the internal dynamics and windows of opportunity in individual nations, and by supporting what is really practical to accomplish. The West cannot, however, "win" by calling for instant change; efforts to impose change from the outside only provide the enemy with fresh ammunition.

Different Priorities

It also cannot win with broad efforts at public diplomacy, regional meetings and initiatives, or with part-time efforts. At least in the case of the United States, it is going to take strong embassy teams that work hard, country by country, and tailor their actions to what can be achieved and what is productive, case by case. Clear national strategies will be needed for military and counterterrorism cooperation and advisory efforts, for supporting balanced political reform at the pace a given nation can accept, and for balancing political reform with economic, social and demographic reform.

Both governments and analysts in the West need to understand that people in the Islamic world do not make politics or Western approaches to human rights their main priority. They are looking for personal security, jobs, education for their children, health care and other government services. The key to defeating Islamic extremism—and the broad popular base that sympathizes with it—comes, first, from providing popular security without oppression and, then, from providing economic opportunity for both today's workers and their children. Survey after survey has shown this. It does not make those in the region who call for political change and sweeping human-rights reforms unimportant; they are voices that will help shape the long-term future of the Islamic world. But, first things first.

Regional policies, meetings and slogans will not deal with real-world needs or provide the kind of dialogue with local officials and reformers, tailored pressure and aid, and country-specific plans and policies that are needed. Strong country teams both in Washington and in U.S. embassies are the keys to success. Quiet, steady advocacy and well-staffed and funded efforts tailored to a given country should replace noisy, episodic, region-wide pressures and demands.

Above all, successful efforts at counterterrorism, reform and public diplomacy must have a national focus. The Arab and Islamic worlds are not monolithic. In fact, country-to-country differences are generally far greater than in the West. Each country requires different kinds of help in counterterrorism and in moving towards reform.

Some countries need help in reforming their political process and enhancing citizen participation; others need help dealing with economic development; still others need special attention to demographic dynamics and population control. The West, therefore, must avoid any generalized strategy of dealing with the Arab-Islamic world as one entity and making policy pronouncements that are as vague as they are unhelpful to local reformers who have been working on their societies for decades.

The United States Should Support, Not Force, Democracy

The U.S. should support those seeking to promote the rule of law, democracy, and human rights in their own countries. Democracy and human-rights activists are the shock troops in the struggle against terrorism, genocide, and nuclear proliferation. But democracy can never be delivered through the barrel of a gun. Assistance to those who are working to build their own democratic societies must be carefully planned and targeted, sustained over time, and based on a thorough understanding of the unique circumstances and profound differences among cultures, religions, and countries. A new U.S. government must work within an international framework, not unilaterally and preemptively, to assist those struggling around the world to bring human rights to their own societies.

John Shattuck,
"Healing Our Self-Inflicted Wounds,"
The American Prospect, *December 17, 2007. www.prospect.org.*

Burden Is on Islamic Nations and Communities

At the same time, this critique of the U.S. and Western approach to winning the long war in no way means that the political, religious and intellectual leaders in Islamic nations do not have to make even more striking changes in their behavior. There is no room for tolerance of inaction or political and religious cowardice within the Islamic world.

The real "war on terrorism" can only be won if the religious, political and intellectual leaders of Islamic countries and communities actively confront and fight neo-Salafi Sunni

Islamist extremism at the religious and ideological level. It will be lost if such leaders stand aside, take half measures, or compromise with enemies that seek to destroy them and what they believe in. It will be lost if they deny that the real issue is the future of Islam, if they tolerate Islamist violence and terrorism when it strikes at unpopular targets like Israel, or if they continue to try to export the blame for their own failures to other nations, religions and cultures.

One message the United States and the West need to firmly communicate to the religious, political and intellectual leaders of Muslim countries and communities is that they cannot be passive or hope to have this struggle won from the outside. No strategy can succeed that is not based on their willingness to take an active role and on their broad acceptance of the fact that this is a war within a religion, not a clash between civilizations. The war to defeat Islamic extremism can only be won at a religious and ideological level if every religious, political and intellectual leader makes the choice to actively engage Islamic extremism rather than engage in cowardice and self-defeat.

Islamic regimes can only win their part of the war if they accept the fact that repression, counterterrorism and the stifling of local reform efforts ultimately aid the very Islamist extremists they are trying to defeat. Algeria, Egypt and Syria have already shown that "long wars" fought on this basis may bring the threat under partial control but cannot defeat it.

If the West has pushed too hard, too quickly, and sometimes for the wrong things, the Muslim or Arab leader who tries to defeat Islamic extremism by blocking or delaying reform or by making concessions to Islamic extremism is guilty of committing self-inflicted wounds to his own faith and country—a failure far worse than any failure of Western states.

The Muslim world is starting to deal with these failures, although several decades after the fact. In December 2005, the Organization of the Islamic Conference met in Mecca and issued a clear statement advocating moderation. The Mecca declaration read in part, "...We reaffirm our unwavering rejection of terrorism and all forms of extremism and violence." In addition, the declaration endorsed the creation of an International Counterterrorism Center to improve global cooperation in the fight against terrorism.

Taking Responsibility at Every Level

The Islamic world, however, must do far more to confront its own failures and stop blaming the West for its self-inflicted wounds. Its leaders must react immediately and decisively every time neo-Salafist terrorists, Islamist Shiites, and other extremist organizations use the Muslim faith as their recruiting platform. While various Muslim leaders have condemned violence against civilians, they have done little to defeat these groups at the ideological level.

Any kind of victory requires a massive additional effort to beat these extremists at their own game by using religious texts and historical facts. Educational and religious reform, use of the media, statements by leaders, sermons, articles, dialogue and intellectual debate are weapons that cannot be ignored. They ultimately will be more important than internal-security forces and counterterrorism campaigns.

The United States has dubbed this struggle a "long war," but this can be a dangerous misnomer. Islamic leaders do not have much time. They confront a world in which Islamic media and the Internet make inaction and attempts at censorship a certain path to losing popular support and seeing extremists gain by default. The religious and ideological struggle needs to be made as short as possible.

Steady progress toward meeting popular needs and goals is equally important. Such progress may often be slow, and change will normally have to be evolutionary, but it must be a constant and publicly credible pursuit that leaders are seen to push forward. Extremists have capitalized on the dissatisfaction of the Arab street and the majority of the Muslim world with their economic and political situation, the steady decay of public services, corruption and the narrow distribution of income. Governments must be more proactive in ensuring personal security, creating jobs, improving education and health care, providing the environment for the private sector to flourish, and ensuring that the rule of law protects property and personal rights.

Increase Tolerance and Pluralism

Islamic regimes also have to at least move towards some form of centrist, moderate political pluralism. Leaders for life, hereditary presidents, one-party systems, and monarchies with captive political parties or none, all have one thing in common. They help breed extremism by denying the rise of moderate Islamic and secular movements that can give local political leaders practical experience and provide a basis for compromise. The tolerance of moderate dissent is another key weapon in the real-world war on terrorism.

The problem is scarcely limited to regimes. Far too many Islamic intellectuals have learned to ignore the candle, live in the dark, and curse the West or outsiders for their plight. They deny the need to shape the future and wallow in the problems of the past. They turn history into a self-inflicted wound and tolerate extremist violence when they perceive it as being directed at their enemies.

Elites in the Muslim world must act on the reality that they cannot survive without contributing to the building of viable civil societies that are sustainable in the long run. Many elites in the Arab and Muslim worlds argue, and rightly so, that the West's push for "democracy" is backfiring. However, they do far too little themselves to provide viable alternatives and put far too much blame for the current level of stagnation on their own governments. An intellectual or businessman who fails to actively help build viable private sectors,

erect educational institutions, and provide employment opportunities for the youth in his own society is little more than
a parasite.

Both leaders and elites need far more willingness to try to
end regional conflicts in ways that actually benefit the peoples
involved. Pretending that the conflicts in Iraq, Afghanistan,
Chechnya, Darfur and Palestine are the problems of others or
are going to solve themselves is not a solution. Blaming the
West and waiting for the United States to solve them is no
better. Holding summits and issuing declarations has not
solved anything for the last 50 years. These conflicts not only
have an impact on their Muslim brethren; they can negatively
affect their own stability. For example, an Iraq torn by civil
war, or disintegrating into three parts, damages not only Iraqis
but the lives of those in every country in the Middle East.

Need for Concerted Action

Terrorism can never be totally eliminated as a tactic, but the
ideology that drives organizations like al-Qaeda can be dis-
credited and its promoters isolated. Support for extremism is
still marginal in Islamic nations. [Osama] Bin Laden and
[Abu Musab] Al-Zarqawi have killed innocent civilians including Arabs and Muslims, have tarred the image of Islam in the
world through suicide bombings and beheadings, and have
destroyed the economies of Iraq and Afghanistan. Poll after
poll has shown that Muslims and Arabs want moderate alternatives to the status quo, if their political, religious and intellectual leaders will actually provide them.

The Islamic world has wasted far too much time com-
plaining about history and too little building the future. Arab
and Muslim governments must understand that; in order to
salvage the image of Islam and insure stability in their countries, they must actively destroy support for Islamist extremism at every level.

The West must join in this struggle, but its role should be to help Islamic nations develop the military and security capabilities they really need and intervene only as allies when absolutely necessary. The West should support long-term sustainable and evolutionary efforts at reform, geared toward helping Islamic nations improve their own economic, political and social systems.

The West must reinforce local reform efforts and avoid being seen as meddling in countries' internal affairs in supporting secular over religious Islamists, driving reform from the outside, or trying to change the character of Muslim countries. It must not be seen as picking sides in the sectarian "game" between Sunnis and Shiites, Arabs and Persians, Afghanis and Pakistanis. To the extent possible, the West must be seen as an even-handed broker in the Arab-Israeli conflict.

Both sides, however, need to get their priorities straight. The key to victory is ultimately in Islamic and not Western hands. Implementing a "winning" strategy in this struggle does require mutual cooperation, but the key lies in the ability of those who are part of the Islamic world to exploit the specific limitations and capabilities of the enemy and defeat them at the heart of their ideological arguments—in the mosques, in the classrooms, on the television screens and at all levels of civil society. This is not the job of Westerners, but of Muslim religious leaders, government officials, business executives and intellectuals.

> *"I felt it was my responsibility to dem-*
> *onstrate that I as a Muslim did not in*
> *any way identify with these morons."*

Muslim Immigrants Should Renounce Terrorist Acts Carried Out in the Name of Islam

Saira Khan

Saira Khan is host of the BBC children's television show, Beat the Boss, *a columnist for* The Daily Mirror, *and the author of the self-help book* P.U.S.H. for Success. *In the following view-point, she recalls her reaction to the July 7, 2005, London transit system bombings. Upon learning that the terrorists were Mus-lims, like her, she felt a personal responsibility to separate herself from them. She asserts that it is the responsibility of moderate Muslims to renounce terrorist acts committed in the name of Is-lam, and of Muslim immigrants in the West to demonstrate loy-alty to their new home country.*

As you read, consider the following questions:

1. What does it mean to "feel British," according to Khan?

2. According to Khan, what causes the hatred and frustration that lead to acts of terrorism?

3. What point about the July 7, 2005, London bombings does Khan feel the British media hasn't gotten across?

I remember exactly what I was doing on the morning of 7 July 2005. My husband Steve and I had a heated discussion after breakfast and he slammed the door very hard when he left for work. I didn't think too much of it until I put the TV on and saw the news. I remember thinking, 'Oh my God, where was Steve's meeting and did he use the Tube?' I started praying for two things: 1. that my husband was OK and alive; and 2. that these incidents [bombings] on the Tube and bus were not connected to Muslims. Only one of my prayers was answered. Steve was fine.

I was devastated to learn that it was Muslim terrorists who carried out the bombings, and furious that these cowards were using my religion to justify their warped and perverse actions. That anger stayed with me. I felt it was my responsibility to demonstrate that I as a Muslim did not in any way identify with these morons. I wanted moderate British Muslims to realise that they could no longer choose to ignore what was happening in their communities; I wanted them to show that they were the majority.

There are, alas, certain Muslim communities here which are not integrated, and the notion of being British does not exist in them. After 7/7, moderate Muslims looked deep within themselves and asked, 'Am I British?' For me, being a British Muslim is very different from being a Muslim brought up anywhere else in the world; I do not share the views about life or the religion of, say, a person who grew up in the Yemen, Saudi Arabia, Syria or Iran. I do not speak Arabic and, furthermore, being a Sunni of Kashmiri origin, I do not wear a burka.

Not only am I British, but I feel British.

Moral Obligations of Muslim Immigrants

By far the most difficult experience of Muslim immigrants in the West has been the aftermath of Muslim acts of political violence in their countries of residence. . . .

What are the moral responsibilities of Muslim minorities under these difficult circumstances? Clearly the first and most important duty of these ethnic groups is to condemn terrorism and do whatever they can to prevent any member of their community from engaging in religiously motivated acts of terror against their host country. Indeed loyalty to the new homeland is the duty of any immigrant.

Nader Habibi, "Moral Obligations of Muslim Immigrants,"
The Arab-American News, *Aug. 26–Sept. 1, 2006.*

The question I put to Muslims who do not feel British—who won't share the British values of tolerance, freedom and democracy—is, 'Why are you living in this country?' This may sound quite harsh, but it is surely a reasonable question.

Feeling British is about more than just speaking English; it's about living the British way of life by participating in British culture.

Being Muslim and British

I feel I have not compromised my Asian roots or my Muslim religion by being British. On the contrary, I am proud that I can speak four Asian languages and have a close bond with my family both here and in Kashmir, but I have not neglected the importance of participating in my country's social and economic culture.

There are parts of Britain where for the past 40 years whole communities have opted out of the British way of life and have lived their 'own' way of life, which includes not speaking English, not having white English friends, not wearing English clothes, not watching English television, not reading English newspapers, not shopping in typical shopping centres and not marrying British people. What frustrates me is that in spite of this lack of integration there are community leaders and politicians who talk about the lack of minority representation in certain areas of mainstream British culture—and some even blame it on discrimination. That may be the case in some instances, but you can hardly have mainstream representation if you have communities that aren't prepared to participate in British culture. I believe that this lack of participation, this isolation, has helped breed the hatred and frustration that have persuaded some to take up terrorism.

My parents came to Britain to work and better their lives, and the best way they could do that was to respect and abide by British values. If I compare my family with families brought up in mainly Muslim communities, I see that we have fared much better in British culture and have not faced the discrimination that they have talked about.

Of course, we do not live in a perfect country. There is still a lot of racism and Islamophobia. Sometimes it is subtly expressed. I can say this because my husband is a white, middle-class Essex man who is well educated, open-minded and has travelled a lot. Before I met him, however, he had no contact with anyone from an ethnic background. What amazed me when I met him was that he had actually studied in Bradford and, while he loved going to the curry house every day with his mates, he could not identify the difference between an Indian or a Pakistani. When I asked him if he knew how to say 'hello' or 'thank you' in Urdu, his reply was, 'I never really thought it was important—they speak English.' My point is that in order to fight terror we all have to become better in-formed and break down the walls of ignorance. As we saw on 7 July, no one is safe from these terrorists. They don't care who they kill, but if, as British people, we cared more about our communities and were more integrated, these terrorists would find it very difficult to operate.

The Duty of Moderate Muslims

Sometimes I feel that the media haven't got across the point that 7 July was just as much of a shock to ordinary law-abiding Muslims as it was to non-Muslims. As the Forest Gate raid [June 2, 2006, anti-terrorism house raid in east London, based on faulty intelligence, in which police shot an innocent Muslim man] demonstrated, not all stereotypical Muslims are terrorists; and you can be British and have a beard and be a moderate Muslim.

I believe that for moderate Muslims there is an important opportunity to demonstrate to the rest of the world exactly how Muslims should live and operate in a Western democracy. On my travels throughout Europe I have not seen the levels of respect, opportunity and freedom given to Muslims that exist in Britain, and sometimes I think that Muslims forget that all too quickly because we have had it so good for so long.

This was recently drummed home by an Afghan taxi-driver who told me that he could not understand the actions of the young Muslim men who demonstrated against the cartoons depicting the Prophet Mohammed and carried placards that clearly said, 'Kill all those who insult Islam.' He told me, 'These kids have never lived in a war zone, they have never been in a country where you are persecuted for your religion and have no rights at all, where there is no support from the government to help you get food, education and healthcare, and where religious tolerance and democracy do not exist. I've managed to come to this country and I feel like I am the luckiest man in the world. I thank God every day for bringing me to this country. I wish I could send some of these young men to Afghanistan and get them to live in my village for a year and see if they would still feel the same way.' As I have said before, it's not up to the government to change the Muslim community; it's up to Muslims. We must face up to the realities of living as British people in a Western democracy in the 21st century.

"*I state here and now that I will not apologize. I did not commit these acts—neither did Saudi Arabia nor the Muslim world.*"

Muslims Should Not Have to Apologize for Terrorist Acts Carried Out in the Name of Islam

Khaled Al-Maeena

In the following viewpoint, Khaled Al-Maeena questions calls for all Muslims to apologize for terrorist attacks committed by a few Muslims. He points to the massacres of Muslims worldwide and asks why there are no similar demands for apologies for these incidents. Placing the blame for terrorism on all Muslims only deepens the divide between Muslims and non-Muslims. In fact, he says, terrorism is a problem affecting all citizens and no one group is to blame. Al-Maeena is the Editor-in-Chief of the Arab News, *the first Saudi English-language daily newspaper.*

Khaled Al-Maeena, "I'm Not Going to Apologize," *Arab News*, July 27, 2005. www.arabnews.com. Copyright © 2005 *Arab News*. All rights reserved. Reproduced by permission.

As you read, consider the following questions:

1. How do anti-Islamists benefit from terrorism committed by Muslims, according to Al-Maeena?
2. Whom does Al-Maeena blame for the hatred and division between the world's peoples?
3. According to Al-Maeena, who is actually deserving of an apology, and why?

"The contrast cannot be more striking. Four Muslims out of millions commit a barbaric crime in London. All the Muslims have been put on the defensive not just in the UK but the world over.

"Three soldiers of the British Army are charged with war crimes. The rallying call goes out that we must all support the army and be sympathetic toward them in this difficult time.

"The pundits were pontificating this morning [July 2005] on Radio 4's Today program, self-assured that these bozos will be tried sympathetically and 'hopefully will be acquitted.' How reassuring! No one is talking of dangerous ideologies being preached among the ranks of Her Majesty's armed forces. No one suspects any cells/schools—dare I say madrasas—teaching the ranks to do unimaginable things. But best of all, no one expects any apologies from any or all of the army.

"One young man from Leeds put it very nicely in a news story filed on the BBC 6 p.m. news last evening: 'I am not going to apologize for this. I condemned this crime, and those who did it did not do so in my name. Why should I be expected to apologize for them?'

"This eloquently sums up the feeling of many of us at a time when most of our community leaders are losing their heads."—Hashim Reza.

This was a letter from Britain. All over the world Muslims are being killed. In Palestine, Israeli forces are using freely supplied American arms to kill children under false pretenses. In Chechnya, Russian forces committed some of the worst atrocities of the past 200 years. The horrific massacres left young boys of eight or nine years with white hair. Young girls were gang raped.

In India, the worst massacres took place in Gujarat where 3,000 Muslims were killed, many of whom were burned alive. The chief minister of Gujarat, the chief of police and other senior officials incited mobs to commit the carnage. Police turned a blind eye as murders and rapes took place. These officials are still in office.

The world recently [July 2005] marked the 10th anniversary of the massacres of Muslims in Srebrenica, where 8,000 Muslim men and boys were shot to death in cold blood over 24 hours by Christian forces right under the eyes of Dutch UN troops. There was not a word or a whisper heard at that time by anyone. In Iraq, America's lethal air power—carelessly aimed cluster bombs and daisycutters that explode above the ground for maximum carnage—killed hundreds of innocent Iraqis who themselves had no love for the tyrant Saddam [Hussein].

The Principle of Collective Guilt

These are but a few examples that could be mentioned. I could go on and on. However, what I would like to ask is why are we told that we have not done enough to condemn the terrorist attacks? Why have not our clerics come out in full force and vilified the perpetrators of terror? They ask us to come out in full force against suicide bombers in Israel. They ask a whole nation to accept the guilt for Sept. 11 [2001 terrorist attacks against the United States]. They ask us to atone and pray for sins committed by our young men. They ask that we wring our hands and show remorse—maybe go a step further and flagellate ourselves. In short, the principle of collective guilt is being applied to Muslims the world over.

In fact, the anti-Islamists delight in such incidents and use it to spread their hatred of Muslims. Julie Burchill's piece in

Spare Us the Apologies

It seems that the Muslim organizations, the media and the so-called moderate Muslims have launched another round of Muslim renunciation of terrorism campaign. That's innocent enough on its face, yet when you think about all of these apologies, you start to wonder if the apologizers don't secretly feel that perhaps Islam did in some way inspire the behavior of the 9/11 hijackers, and you start worrying that all of these apologies might cause others to openly believe the same. Let me take this opportunity to assure everyone that Islam did not inspire 9/11, and to ask Muslim leaders to spare the rest of us the bi-annual ritual of Muslim apology for 9/11.... Let me add that terrorism is not an Islamic phenomenon. It is an act of violence that is carried out against innocent civilians to achieve political aims.

Anisa Abd el Fattah, "Vindicating Islam,"
The Arab-American News, Aug. 11–17, 2007.

the July 16th [2005] issue of *The Times*, London, didn't miss a jab against Saudi Arabia—accusing the Saudi authorities of not even allowing the British troops to celebrate St. Valentine's Day.

Ignorance reaches new heights.

However, I state here and now that I will not apologize. I did not commit these acts—neither did Saudi Arabia nor the Muslim world. Individual acts should not be blamed on our Ummah, and we must be brave and not listen to PR companies and acquiesce. Let us be brave and stand tall. Our religion is a religion of peace, and it is we Muslims who have been both slain and slandered in the past few decades.

Yes, we are against terror at home or abroad. But those who accuse us should also understand that terrorism exists everywhere. In some countries there is state-sponsored terrorism. And as for the apologies I have not read one apology for the massacres of Muslims. It would be understandable to say "Let them apologize to us first." But humanity needs to move beyond that.

Stop Placing Blame

The media, be it British or American or Arab, needs to curb the subjective drivel that spawns hatred and division and get back to the business of seeking the truth—and objectively reporting it. And let us all stop asking one another to take the blame for the problems that plague all of mankind.

With this realization, the only apologies that would need to be made would be to those whose lives could have been saved were we all working together to solve these serious problems rather than blaming one another for them.

It is time for all the peoples of the world to tell murdering terrorists, marauding armies and hate mongering media moguls "We have had enough." And none of us need to apologize.

| *"It is vital to question if we—Muslims— should lay the blame on others for Islamophobia or if we should first look hard at ourselves."*

Muslims Should Examine Roots of Terrorism Within Islam Before Blaming Others

Tawfik Hamid

Tawfik Hamid is a former member of the Islamic extremist group Jamma'a Islameia and is now a Muslim reformer who serves on the Advisory Board of the Intelligence Summit. In this viewpoint, Hamid criticizes Muslim organizations that regularly accuse non-Muslims of "Islamophobia" without examining the causes of such fear. Instead, he says, Muslims should take a look at which aspects of their own society and religion cause so much violence today, before they lay all the blame on others. He calls for Muslims to condemn terrorism committed by Muslims, just as they condemn discrimination against Muslims.

As you read, consider the following questions:

1. Why did the Council of American-Islamic Relations accuse Rep. Peter King of encouraging Islamophobia?

2. What kinds of reforms does Hamid believe Islam needs to undergo?

3. Who are the most common murderers of Muslims, according to Hamid?

Islamic organizations regularly accuse non-Muslims of "Islamophobia," a fear and disdain for everything Islamic. On May 17 [2007], this accusation bubbled up again as foreign ministers from the Organization of the Islamic Conference called Islamophobia "the worst form of terrorism." These ministers also warned, according to the *Arab News*, that this form of discrimination would cause millions of Muslims in Western countries, "may of whom were already underprivileged," to be "further alienated."

In America, perhaps the most conspicuous organization to persistently accuse opponents of Islamophobia is the Council of American-Islamic Relations [CAIR]. CAIR has taken up the legal case of the "Flying Imams," the six individuals who were pulled from a US Airways flight in Minneapolis this past November [2006] after engaging in suspicious behavior before takeoff. Not long ago, [March 2007] CAIR filed a "John Doe" lawsuit that would have made passengers liable for "malicious" complaints about suspicious Muslim passengers.

In an interview at the time, CAIR spokesman Nihad Awad accused Rep. Peter King (R., N.Y.) of being an "extremist" who "encourages Islamophobia" for pointing out what most people would think is obvious, that such a lawsuit would have a chilling effect on passengers who witnessed alarming activity and wished to report it. We can only assume that Mr. Awad believes flyers should passively remain in a state of fear as they travel and submissively risk their lives. In this case, Congress is acting appropriately and considering passing a law sponsored by Mr. King that would grant passengers immunity from such lawsuits.

It may seem bizarre, but Islamic reformers are not immune to the charge of "Islamophobia" either. For 20 years I have preached a reformed interpretation of Islam that teaches peace and respects human rights. I have consistently spoken out—with dozens of other Muslim and Arab reformers—against the mistreatment of women, gays and religious minorities in the Islamic world. We have pointed out the violent teachings of Salafism and the imperative of Westerners to protect themselves against it.

Yet according to CAIR's Michigan spokeswoman, Zeinab Chami, I am "the latest weapon in the Islamophobe arsenal." If standing against the violent edicts of Shariah law is "Islamophobic," then I will treat her accusation as a badge of honor.

Take a Look at Ourselves First

Muslims must ask what prompts this "phobia" in the first place. When we in the West examine the worldwide atrocities perpetrated daily in the name of Islam, it is vital to question if we—Muslims—should lay the blame on others for Islamophobia or if we should first look hard at ourselves.

According to a recent Pew Global Attitudes survey, "younger Muslims in the U.S. are much more likely than older Muslim Americans to say that suicide bombing in the defense of Islam can be at least sometimes justified." About one out of every four American Muslims under 30 think suicide bombing in defense of Islam is justified in at least some circumstances. Twenty-eight percent believe that Muslims did not carry out the 9/11 attacks [2001 terrorist attacks against the United States] and 32% declined to answer that question.

While the survey has been represented in the media as proof of moderation among American Muslims, the actual results should yield the opposite conclusion. If, as the Pew study estimates, there are 2.35 million Muslims in America, that means there are a substantial number of people in the U.S.

Free Speech About Islam Is Under Attack

Many times, groups like the Council on American-Islamic Relations have classified true statements about Islam and jihad as "hateful." ... We are now in danger, under the guise of forbidding "hate speech," of forbidding discussion of the reality of Islamic jihad at precisely the moment that Islamic supremacists are pressing forward as never before with their program of stealth jihad against the West.

Robert Spencer,
"The Jihad Against Free Speech,"
Human Events, *June 17, 2008. www.humanevents.com.*

who think suicide bombing is sometimes justified. Similarly, if 5% of American Muslims support al Qaeda, that's more than 100,000 people.

To bring an end to Islamophobia, we must employ a holistic approach that treats the core of the disease. It will not suffice to merely suppress the symptoms. It is imperative to adopt new Islamic teachings that do not allow killing apostates (Redda Law). Islamic authorities must provide mainstream Islamic books that forbid polygamy and beating women. Accepted Islamic doctrine should take a strong stand against slavery and the raping of female war prisoners, as happens in Darfur under the explicit canons of Shariah ("Ma Malakat Aimanikum"). Muslims should teach, everywhere and universally, that a woman's testimony in court counts as much as a man's, that women should not be punished if they marry whom they please or dress as they wish.

We Must Rescue Our Religion

We Muslims should publicly show our strong disapproval for the growing number of attacks by Muslims against other faiths and against other Muslims. Let us not even dwell on 9/11, Madrid, London, Bali and countless other scenes of carnage. It has been estimated that of the two million refugees fleeing Islamic terror in Iraq, 40% are Christian, and many of them seek a haven in Lebanon, where the Christian population itself has declined by 60%. Even in Turkey, Islamists recently found it necessary to slit the throats of three Christians for publishing Bibles.

Of course, Islamist attacks are not limited to Christians and Jews. Why do we hear no Muslim condemnation of the ongoing slaughter of Buddhists in Thailand by Islamic groups? Why was there silence over the Mumbai train bombings which took the lives of over 200 Hindus in 2006? We must not forget that innocent Muslims, too, are suffering. Indeed, the most common murderers of Muslims are, and have always been, other Muslims. Where is the Muslim outcry over the Sunni-Shiite violence in Iraq?

Islamophobia could end when masses of Muslims demonstrate in the streets against videos displaying innocent people being beheaded with the same vigor we employ against airlines, Israel and cartoons of Muhammad. It might cease when Muslims unambiguously and publicly insist that Shariah law should have no binding legal status in free, democratic societies.

It is well past time that Muslims cease using the charge of "Islamophobia" as a tool to intimidate and blackmail those who speak up against suspicious passengers and against those who rightly criticize current Islamic practices and preachings. Instead, Muslims must engage in honest and humble introspection. Muslims should—must—develop strategies to rescue our religion by combating the tyranny of Salafi Islam and its dreadful consequences. Among more important outcomes, this will also put an end to so-called Islamophobia.

"We need to learn to listen to our young
men and women and pay attention to
their grievances."

Muslim Organizations Need to Better Address Issues and Concerns Relevant to Young Muslims

Ziauddin Sardar

*In the following viewpoint, Ziauddin Sardar discusses the senti-
ment among many British Muslims that Muslim organizations,
including mosques, are not speaking to the needs of young Muslims. The marginalization of young Muslims by mainstream
Muslim communities, Sardar argues, pushes them toward extremist organizations, which are more welcoming of young
people. To stop this trend, more government oversight over Muslim organizations is needed to ensure that they are run in a
more democratic and representative fashion. Sardar is a British
Muslim intellectual and the author of* Desperately Seeking Paradise: Journeys of a Skeptical Muslim.

Ziauddin Sardar, "Beyond Blame and Shame: What We Must Do Now," *New Statesman*,
vol. 18, no. 869, July 25, 2005, pp. 18–19. www.newstatesman.com. Copyright © 2005
New Statesman, Ltd. Reproduced by permission.

As you read, consider the following questions:

1. According to Sardar, why is the Charity Commission not the most appropriate government entity for regulating British mosques?

2. How does Ehsan Masood feel the Koran should be taught differently than it is currently taught in British madrasas?

3. Why is it difficult for young British Muslims to develop relationships with their parents, according to Dr. Rabia Malik?

"What are we going to do?" This is the question Muslims are asking in hastily arranged meetings and conferences throughout Britain. There is a strong indication that Muslims are going beyond self-justificatory and self-satisfied Islamic rhetoric to recognising the problems of the reality of Muslim life in Britain. Beyond the obvious answers—"we must fight to ensure that Britain changes its foreign policy"—there are some surprisingly practical suggestions.

The emerging consensus is well articulated by Dr Iftikhar Malik, professor of history at Bath Spa University College. "It is time," he says, "to go beyond the blame-and-shame game and develop an accountable culture that brings our frustrated and alienated youth in from the cold." An entire class of angry youth, working as well as middle class, has emerged from among Britain's Muslims. "So far," Malik also says, "nobody is talking about younger women. They are just as angry as young men."

We need to learn to listen to our young men and women and pay attention to their grievances.

A great deal of attention is focused on the lack of accountability in the Muslim community. There is a widespread perception that imams, mosque leaders and spokespeople for Muslim organisations, such as the Muslim Council of Britain and Muslim Association of Britain, are unrepresentative and unelected. "Around 70 per cent of the Muslim population in Britain is between 14 and 34. Yet the average age of the so-called leaders that Tony Blair [British Prime Minister until 2007] met after the London bombs [in June 2005] is well over 50," says the novelist and playwright Suhayl Saadi. This unrepresentative and unaccountable culture needs to be "challenged, subverted and debunked. We need to expose the pornographies of our imams and preachers, tear off the petty emperors' robes, and get down on the Muslim street to seed sane and rational ideas of liberation which combat nihilistic exclusion and psychotic exclusivism," he says.

Stop Marginalizing Youth

The conventional Muslim leaderships, both of mosques and community organisations, have totally marginalised young people. Indeed, suggests Muddassar Ahmed, founder of the Muslim Public Affairs Committee UK (MPACUK), our leaders fear young people. They cannot relate to them, and feel threatened. "It's only when young people feel they can voice their frustrations about the community within the community that a large part of their anger will dissipate," Ahmed says.

Our mosques are largely tribal, and controlled by old men on the dole with no understanding of the changing world around them, says Asim Siddiqui of City Circle. Young people are often banned from discussing controversial issues at the mosque—not just issues of British foreign policy but also such urgent matters as the increasing drug addiction among young Muslims, or the belief of a number of Muslim social scientists that most single mothers in London are Muslim. The unwelcoming and suffocating atmosphere within mosques forces young people towards extremist organisations which are more welcoming. The situation is made worse by some mosques and Islamic centres in Britain being controlled by groups that supported and participated in the "Afghan jihad". These groups actively seek disenfranchised young people for initiation in jihadi ideology.

What this means is that the management and administration of mosques needs better regulatory oversight. As a matter of urgency, says Ahmed, the government should insist that all mosque trusts and committees reorganise themselves and bring young people into their management and administrative structures. At least half the membership of each committee should consist of young people and women. But this in itself is not good enough. In the long term, we need an independent body, supported by the government, with a specific mandate to ensure that mosques are run democratically, their trustees and leaders are made accountable, and women and the young are represented adequately. At present, mosques in Britain are regulated by the Charity Commission, which is good, but not geared to the specific functions of a mosque. "Mosques are public places," says Ehsan Masood, a journalist, "yet they have been allowed to mushroom with very little external help." There aren't many other countries in which mosques are left to manage themselves.

Change Cultural Institutions

The syllabuses of madrasas—traditional Islamic schools, often attached to a mosque—also need attention from an Ofsted-type [England's office for standards in education] body. "Tens of thousands of kids spend two hours every evening rote-learning the Koran," Masood points out. "But the Koran needs to be taught to children in its historical context; rote learning of Arabic letters often leads to closed minds that are ripe for exploitation by the extremists."

Imams have received a heavy battering over the past two weeks [since the July 7, 2005, London transit system bombings]. There seems to be unanimous agreement that imams imported from Pakistan Bangladesh and the Middle East, who do not speak English and know little about British culture, are a particular problem. "We need to end the cruel practice of employing under-educated, underpaid and overworked imported imams," says Ahmed. As a matter of urgency, suggests Malik, existing imams should be required to go through crash courses in English, politics, history and sociology. In the long run we need home-grown facilities for training suitable imams.

Two other Muslim institutions also need to change—faith schools and charities. Muslim faith schools, while doing an admirable job, often engender the mentality of exclusiveness in their pupils. "I fear," says AbdoolKarim Vakil, chair of the Muslim Institute's Brainstorming Symposium, "that they are not producing rounded individuals who can relate to broader British culture." The only way for such schools to promote healthy multiculturalism is if they have a large non-Muslim intake. Vakil suggests that it should be mandatory for Muslim schools to accept at least 20 per cent of their pupils from other faith groups.

Muslim charities need to modify their funding priorities. With the past decade has come the emergence of numerous Muslim charities. Many of these, such as Islamic Relief and Muslim Aid, are very successful at raising money. On the whole they are well managed, dynamic institutions. They exclusively support foreign projects however. "But charity begins at home," says Siddiqui of City Circle, "and our successful charities also need to pay attention to the plight of the Muslim community." They should specifically target local causes and provide much-needed support for them. "I would suggest that at least half of the charitable funds should be allocated to causes in Britain, such as youth projects, as well as arts and theatre, and supporting students taking up careers in journalism or seeking to become imams," says Siddiqui.

Community Action

There are a number of other areas where individual or collective action is needed. The middle class needs to address the issue of educational standards among Muslims with a real pas-

Young Muslims: More Observant, More Radical

	Age	
	18–29	30+
Religion	%	%
Attend mosque...		
Weekly or more	50	35
Few times a month or year	24	26
Seldom/never	26	39
	100	100
Conflict between devout faith & modern life...		
Yes, conflict	42	28
Not in conflict	54	67
DK/Refused	4	5
	100	100
Think of self as:		
Muslim first	60	41
American first	25	30
Both equally	10	22
Neither/other/DK	5	7
	100	100
Radicalism		
Suicide bombing:		
Justified	15	6
Not Justified	80	85
DK/Refused	5	9
	100	100
View of al Qaeda..		
Favorable	7	4
Unfavorable	74	67
DK/Refused	19	29
	100	100

TAKEN FROM: Pew Research Center, *Muslim Americans: Middle Class and Mostly Mainstream*, May 22, 2007. http://people-press.org.

sion. Concerned Muslims should be mentoring underachieving individuals and participating in the raising of educational standards by greater involvement in the educational process—for example, by joining school governing boards; by encouraging and helping underachieving youths find suitable vocational training programmes; and by emphasising the value of education in Islam.

"Anyone distributing extremist literature needs to be dealt with swiftly by the community," says Masood. "If the Tory party won't tolerate the BNP [British National Party] outside its party headquarters, Muslims should have no hesitation in expelling unreconstructed extremists handing out inflammatory literature outside our mosques."

We also need to make a start on repairing the gap between parents and children in Asian Muslim communities. There is often little emotional intimacy between the generations, with the result that parents don't know what their children are thinking, feeling and doing. "Young Muslims have to negotiate their lives in a totally different context to their parents," says Dr Rabia Malik, a family therapist and academic. This makes it difficult for them to develop a relationship with their parents, whose traditional habits and lifestyles they often despise. The parents themselves are very conscious of their status and see admitting failure as a shame. "Most Muslim parents," says Malik, "are in denial about the activities of their children. They have wrapped themselves with a mythology that everything is hunky-dory."

The first step to bridging this emotional divide is for young people to talk among themselves about living in two different contexts. "We need to create spaces within our community where young people, male and female, can meet freely to talk about their problems," says Malik. This is where most of their frustrations could be aired. And, somehow, we need to communicate to the parents that there is nothing shameful about talking honestly about their problems. Ultimately, the Muslim community will be respected only if it is honest to itself and pursues a culture of excellence. "We must learn to see ourselves as we really are, as well as learn to help ourselves," says Siddiqui.

A Window of Opportunity

In truth, none of these debates or proposed solutions is new. They are not the product of 7 July, but have been raised for several years. Yet the atrocities in London offer a window of opportunity to translate debate into action. We must recognise one significant fact, however. Many of these thoughts preparatory to policy changes and programmes of action will demand creative new links with government agencies. And that makes Iraq a factor both in the creation of the problem and in engineering a solution. Muslims must be able to negotiate change and retain their rightful democratic freedom to oppose UK government policy on Iraq; free to connect the dots of their concern. Greater democracy, accountability and transparency within the Muslim community are their demands. They demand no less of their elected government.

> *"A new ecumenical paradigm of dialogue might be found in the historical relations of the three monotheistic sister religions."*

Christian, Jewish, and Muslim Leaders Must Communicate with Each Other to Fight Religious Extremism

Ghassan Rubeiz

Ghassan Rubeiz is a Middle East analyst and the former secretary for the Geneva-based World Council of Churches for the Middle East. In the following viewpoint, he discusses the value of interfaith dialogue among Christians, Muslims, and Jews, as a means to fight religious extremism. He emphasizes that this must be done with respect for all beliefs and empathy for others' experiences. Highlighting the many barriers to interfaith dialogue, including globalization, Rubeiz suggests that the historical roots of all three religions might be the best places to begin an interfaith dialogue.

Ghassan Rubeiz, "Changes Needed to Facilitate Reconciliation," *Arab American News*, vol. 22, no. 1080, October 21–27, 2006, p. 9. Copyright © 2006 *Arab American News*. Reproduced by permission.

As you read, consider the following questions:

1. Why are religious authorities often afraid of the process of questioning scriptures, according to Rubeiz?
2. Why does globalization pose a barrier to interfaith dialogue, in Rubeiz's view?
3. According to Rubeiz, for what is the modern Christian church often criticized today?

Christianity, Judaism and Islam have a great challenge to limit the growing sectarian tension that fuels low intensity conflict as well as full scale wars. Is interfaith dialogue relevant to local and international bridge making? Interfaith dialogue is a search for common grounds in truth, values and interests.

But there are rules for dialogue and there is practice for wisdom. To start with, local respect for expertise is paramount. It is assumed that the most credible experts on Islam are Muslims and the same for other religions. To illustrate, Pope Benedict [XVI] has defined jihad in Islam in a simplistic way. The dominant writing of Western experts on Arabs and on Islam is too subjective and often negative.

Interfaith dailogue requires living experience in other cultures and positive sharing in the environment of other faiths. No amount of sophistication in theology or academia is a substitute for experiencing genuine contact with other cultures and religions.

Dialogue is not about scoring points or moving people away from their beliefs. The focus is not to teach but to learn, not to impress but to empathize and identify with the other. Dialogue requires personal authenticity, active listening, warm non-verbal communication and subtle linguistic exchange.

More rules. No faith is excluded as unworthy of dialogue, including people outside monotheism and even "non believers." The point is that spirituality is not the monopoly of people of dogma.

Religion as a Catalyst for Peace

There appears to be considerable truth to the oft-heard claim that Christian-Muslim co-existence must be achieved lest our collective future turn out brief and brutal. Which is why it might appear outrageous to suggest, as I'm about to do, that religion may also be just the catalyst we need to steer us clear of the apparent collision course.

Religion—a solution to the problem of religiously motivated conflict and violence? Yes, actually. Because in their best traditions, the world's two dominant faiths do promote peace, both through their central teachings and the lessons-by-example taught every day by innumerable Muslims and Christians who take their scriptures seriously.

Tom Krattenmaker, "Religion Can Help End Wars, Too,"
USA Today, July 14, 2008. http://blogs.usatoday.com.

Dialogue enthusiasts in Christianity and Islam are expected to discourage their colleagues from campaigns of proselytism. Put differently, extreme evangelists are not in the business of dialogue. Extremists of all religions consider interfaith dialogue misguided. Also, interfaith contact is not welcomed in communities of restricted freedom.

Dialogue is hard work, but when there is progress the participants get on a spiritual "high." Often, what makes dialogue frigid are its agents; too much dialogue has been assigned to celebrities, politicians or hard line religious authorities.

Barriers to Dialogue

Dialogue agencies have been frustrated in their work. The reasons for failure of interfaith dialogue are complex. Superiority stands out. Around the world, at an early age, children are taught that their God is the best there is. Other people's Gods are often suspect or imperfect. Ironically, as a result of narrow minded religious pedagogy, people end up worshipping three distinct Monotheist Gods. There is an articulated and paralyzing fear and possessiveness among high power religious and political authorities that the process of questioning the scripture leads to the unraveling of the basic system of faith; and chaos is the outcome.

Moreover, in a world of growing political turmoil, extremists "steal the show." While conservatives slow dialogue due to the fear of unraveling, radical political groups create inter religious tension that makes the social climate of dialogue hostile. Terrorists "dialogue" with violence, seeking inter religious contact. Moderate preachers do not receive their share of media's attention. Violence in religion comes also in much more subtle ways. In the West, some churches run an industry of fear and anxiety, praying for end time war and proliferating inflammatory rhetoric about other religions and civilizations.

Another dialogue barrier is globalization. Sermons' fire and fury are no longer addressed primarily to the local church or the local mosque. What a Western priest says about Islam and Muslims in Chicago is heard in Cairo and New Delhi the same day. Similarly, angry Muslim preachers in Kashmir or Karachi address Christians around the globe through cable channels. Real wars are nowadays fought on the international screen. The summer [2006] war in Lebanon and Israel fueled religious hatred around the world.

Finally, among barriers to dialogue is the fluctuating relation of the center to the extreme in religious communities. The lines between moderation and extremes are often hazy and depending on the level of insecurity of the community and who decides what is mainline. The trend is for each religious community to affirm moderation and distance itself from extremists. Mainline Christians distance themselves from extreme Evangelicals. Similarly, Muslims distance themselves from suicide bombers who target civilians. But still, non Muslims complain to moderate Muslims that they are not loud enough in their criticism of their extreme side. Reciprocally, Muslims ask Christians to watch extreme Evangelicals who are growing in influence in Western society. For their side, Jewish dialogue spokespersons are often challenged to listen hard to Palestinian suffering.

A New Paradigm

Practical dialogue has proven to be more effective than formal theological dialogue. Over the last two centuries immense religious resources have been used overseas to advance the well being of people through education, health and development projects. Egalitarian partnerships between donors and local community leaders transform foreign aid from a charity to a process of empowerment.

An alternative opportunity for reconciliation among monotheistic religions may lie at their historical roots, and not in their strategies of moderation. Religious institutions, like all social structures, tend over the passage of time to lose some of the core values of their original tenants. Early Christianity has carried the torch of unconditional love, forgiveness and personal spiritual renewal. Christianity has best been exemplified by the life of Jesus of Nazareth. But over the years, Christianity has been Hellenized, then Europeanized, and in recent centuries, due to proliferation of televangelism, it has become too Americanized. Critics of the modern church today observe an institution that is too burdened with dogma and too distant from original Christian tenants.

Institutional Islam, on the other hand, has not escaped the impact of politics. It is surprising to observe today that Muslims are so conflicted about freedom of interpretation of their faith. To what extent is the dominant fear of open interpretation of the Word in Islam an artifact of politics?

In sum, a new ecumenical paradigm of dialogue might be found in the historical relations of the three monotheistic sister religions rather [than] in their adapting of their contemporary hierarchies. A new era of interfaith dialogue requires the birth of a new framework of teaching religion, a new way to practice dialogue and an affirmative perspective of the complementarities of faiths.

Periodical Bibliography

The following articles have been selected to supplement the diverse views presented in this chapter.

Thomas L. Friedman	"If It's a Muslim Problem, It Needs a Muslim Solution," *The New York Times*, July 8, 2005.
Laurie Goodstein	"Muslim Leaders Confront Terror Threat Within Islam," *The New York Times*, Sept. 2, 2005.
Raja Kamal and Rosanne Model	"The Need for Smart Muslim Charities," *Chicago Tribune*, Dec. 2, 2004.
Saira Khan	"We Are Up Against 20 Years of Planning," *The Spectator*, July 7, 2007.
Rami G. Khouri	"West Needs to Better Assess Islam," *The Arab American News*, Apr. 12–18, 2008.
Don Oldenburg	"Muslims' Unheralded Messenger: Antiterrorism Group Founder Hopes to Rally a Crowd," *The Washington Post*, May 13, 2005.
Mary Beth Sheridan	"Educating Against Extremism: Muslims Reach Out to Youths Who Could Be Susceptible to Radicalism," *The Washington Post*, Aug. 8, 2005.
Larry B. Stammer	"Homegrown Risk Worries U.S. Muslims," *Los Angeles Times*, July 25, 2005.
Mercedes Stephenson	"Hitting Home," *Chatelaine*, Sept. 2006.
Daniel Treiman	"Moderate Muslims Seek Foothold in U.S.," *Forward*, June 17, 2005.
Stephen Vincent	"Where Are the Moderate Muslims?" *The American Enterprise*, April/May 2005.
Abdurrahman Wahid	"Right Islam vs. Wrong Islam," *The Wall Street Journal*, Dec. 30, 2005.

For Further Discussion

Chapter 1

1. The viewpoints in this chapter are part of a larger question of whether Islamic militancy is an ideology rooted in Islamic culture and beliefs, or whether it is an ideology in response to specific political and economic circumstances. After reading the viewpoints in this chapter, do you believe either one of these overarching factors adequately explains Islamic militancy?

2. Former British Prime Minister Tony Blair's argument that Islamic militancy is a rejection of Western values echoes former President George W. Bush's explanation after the terrorist attacks on the United States on September 11, 2001. After reading the other viewpoints in this chapter, do you find this explanation persuasive? Explain your answer.

Chapter 2

1. Much of the discussion of whether the Qur'an condones terrorism comes back to the variety of ways the Qur'an can be—and is—interpreted. How does this discussion compare with those you've heard about other holy books, such as the Bible and the Torah?

2. Ziauddin Sardar argues that English-language editions of the Qur'an distorted that book intentionally, in order to malign the Muslim faith. Do you believe his argument, or do you think the Qur'an's mistranslation was accidental?

3. To what extent do you think it is moderate Muslims' responsibility to educate non-Muslims about Muslim beliefs and the Qur'an? To what extent is it non-Muslims' responsibility to educate themselves?

Chapter 3

1. Do you find the arguments of Rod Liddle and Melanie Phillips, that Western governments' tolerance for and engagement with Islamic militancy have encouraged its expansion, convincing? If so, how do you think these governments should combat Islamic militancy?

2. John F. Kavanaugh and Zeyno Baran disagree about whether Western governments should work with Islamic militant groups, while Robert Spencer suggests Western governments should work with moderate Muslim groups. Do you believe Western governments should reach out to any Muslim groups? If so, what do you believe should be the qualifying criteria for whether or not Western governments negotiate with these groups?

Chapter 4

1. Do you agree with Anthony H. Cordesman, that Islamic militancy can be defeated only by Muslims themselves? Or do you believe Western governments should play a role in defeating it as well?

2. The disagreement about whether Muslims are obligated to renounce terrorism, represented by viewpoints by Saira Khan and Khaled Al-Maeena, has broader implications. To what extent do you think it is the responsibility of members of a group to renounce despicable acts by other members?

Organizations to Contact

The editors have compiled the following list of organizations concerned with the issues debated in this book. The descriptions are derived from materials provided by the organizations. All have publications or information available for interested readers. The list was compiled on the date of publication of the present volume; the information provided here may change. Be aware that many organizations take several weeks or longer to respond to inquiries, so allow as much time as possible.

American Foreign Policy Council (AFPC)
509 C Street NE, Washington, DC   20002
(202) 543-1006 • fax: (202) 543-1007
Web site: www.afpc.org

The American Foreign Policy Council is a nonprofit organization that provides information and analysis to those who make or influence American foreign policy. AFPC also assists world leaders, particularly in the former Soviet Union, in building democracies. It publishes regular bulletins, including *Foreign Policy Alert, Asia Security Monitor* and *Eurasia Security Watch.*

American Israel Public Affairs Committee (AIPAC)
251 H Street NW, Washington, DC   20001
(202) 639-5200
Web site: www.aipac.org

The American Israel Public Affairs Committee is a pro-Israel lobbying group. It works with both Democratic and Republican leaders to promote policies that strengthen the U.S.-Israel relationship and promote Israel's security. AIPAC publishes *Near East Report, Middle East Spotlight, Israel Connection, Defense Digest,* and other publications.

Center for Strategic and International Studies (CSIS)
1800 K Street NW, Washington, DC 20006
(202) 887-0200 • fax: (202) 775-3199
Web site: www.csis.org

The Center for Strategic and International Studies is a bipartisan nonprofit organization seeking to advance global security and prosperity. It serves as a planning partner for government officials in its research, analysis, and policy initiatives. It publishes numerous reports such as *The Evolving Security Situation in Iraq: The Continuing Need for Strategic Patience, Currents and Crosscurrents of Radical Islam*, and the *Transnational Threats Update.*

Council on American-Islamic Relations (CAIR)
453 New Jersey Avenue SE, Washington, DC 20003
(202) 488-8787 • fax: (202) 488-0833
e-mail: info@cair.com
Web site: www.cair.com

CAIR is a nonprofit grassroots civil rights and advocacy group that works to promote greater understanding of Islam and to protect the civil liberties of Muslim Americans. CAIR conducts research, counsels and advocates for Muslim Americans, organizes lobbying efforts, and provides education. Its publications include *An Employer's Guide to Islamic Religious Practices, An Educator's Guide to Islamic Religious Practices*, and *Law Enforcement Official's Guide to the Muslim Community*, as well as an annual report on the status of American Muslim civil rights.

Council on Foreign Relations (CFR)
The Harold Pratt House, 58 East 68th Street
New York, NY 10065
(212) 434-9400 • fax: (212) 434-9800
Web site: www.cfr.org

The Council on Foreign Relations is a nonpartisan think tank that acts as a resource to help government officials, citizens, students, educators, and others better understand the world and the foreign policy decisions facing the United States. It provides current information and analyses of world events and American foreign policy and supports a Studies Program that promotes independent research. The Council does not take institutional positions on policy matters. It publishes the journal *Foreign Affairs*, newsletters *Daily Brief* and *The World This Week*, task force reports, and numerous other publications.

Foundation for Middle East Peace (FMEP)

1761 N Street NW, Washington, DC 20036
(202) 835-3650 • fax: (202) 835-3651
e-mail: info@fmep.org
Web site: www.fmep.org

The Foundation for Middle East Peace is a nonprofit organization that promotes peace between Israel and Palestine. FMEP offers speakers, sponsors programs, and makes small grants. It publishes the *Report on Israeli Settlement in the Occupied Territories* and other reports, such as *Building Sovereignty in Palestine—A New Paradigm for the Gaza-Egypt Frontier.*

Middle East Forum

1500 Walnut Street, Suite 1050, Philadelphia, PA 19102
(215) 546-5406 • fax: (215) 546-5409
e-mail: info@meforum.org
Web site: www.meforum.org

The Middle East Forum is a think tank that promotes American interests—such as fighting radical Islam and working for Palestinian acceptance of Israel—in the Middle East. It actively urges policies that protect Americans and their allies in this region and educates the public about Middle East issues and policy. The Forum publishes the *Middle East Quarterly* journal and special reports, such as *Asymmetrical Threat Concept and Its Reflections on International Security.*

U.S. Department of Homeland Security
Washington, DC   20528
(202) 282-8000
Web site: www.dhs.gov

The U.S. Department of Homeland Security was established in 2001 to provide a unifying core for the national network of organizations and institutions working to secure the United States. It assesses the nation's vulnerabilities, coordinates with other organizations to ensure the most effective response, and provides information to the American public and state and local governments. The Department publishes annual performance reports, privacy impact assessments, and other reports.

U.S. Department of State
2201 C Street NW, Washington, DC   20520
(202) 647-4000
Web site: www.state.gov

The U.S. Department of State represents the United States in its relationships with foreign governments, organizations, and individuals. It seeks to promote a more free, prosperous, and secure world. The Department publishes *Diplomacy: The U.S. State Department at Work*, as well as country reports on human rights practices, country reports on terrorism, and various other publications.

Washington Institute for Near East Policy
1828 L Street NW, Suite 1050, Washington, DC   20036
(202) 452-0650 • fax: (202) 223-5364
Web site: www.washingtoninstitute.org

The Washington Institute for Near East Policy is an organization devoted to the advancement of a balanced and realistic understanding of American interests in the Middle East. Led by a bipartisan board of advisors, the Institute promotes American engagement in the Middle East that is committed to strengthening alliances and friendships and promoting security, peace, prosperity, and democracy for the people in that region. The Institute publishes policy papers, military research papers, research notes, and other publications.

Bibliography of Books

Khaled M.
Abou Al Fadl
The Great Theft: Wrestling Islam from the Extremists. New York: HarperOne, 2005.

Schmuel Bar
Warrant for Terror: The Fatwas of Militant Islam, and the Duty of Jihad. Lanham, MD: Rowman & Littlefield, 2006.

Bruce Bawer
Surrender: Appeasing Islam, Sacrificing Freedom. New York: Doubleday, 2009.

Bruce Bawer
While Europe Slept: How Radical Islam Is Destroying the West from Within. New York: Doubleday, 2006.

Daniel Benjamin
and Steven Simon
The Age of Sacred Terror: Radical Islam's War Against America. New York: Random House, 2002.

Mark Bowden
Guests of the Ayatollah: The First Battle in America's War with Militant Islam. New York: Atlantic Monthly Press, 2006.

Dinesh D'Souza
The Enemy At Home: The Cultural Left and Its Responsibility for 9/11. New York: Doubleday, 2007.

Faisal Devji
The Terrorist in Search of Humanity: Militant Islam and Global Politics. New York: Columbia University Press, 2008.

John L. Esposito — *Unholy War: Terror in the Name of Islam.* New York: Oxford University Press USA, 2002.

Brigitte Gabriel — *Because They Hate: A Survivor of Islamic Terror Warns America.* New York: St. Martin's Press, 2006.

Brigitte Gabriel — *They Must Be Stopped: Why We Must Defeat Radical Islam and How We Can Do It.* New York: St. Martin's Press, 2008.

Lee Harris — *The Suicide of Reason: Radical Islam's Threat to the West.* New York: Basic Books, 2007.

David Horowitz — *Unholy Alliance: Radical Islam and the American Left.* Washington, DC: Regnery Publishing, 2004.

Ed Husain — *The Islamist.* New York: Penguin Global, 2008.

Zahid Hussain — *Frontline Pakistan: The Struggle with Militant Islam.* New York: Columbia University Press, 2007.

Ayesha Jalal — *Partisans of Allah: Jihad in South Asia.* Cambridge, MA: Harvard University Press, 2008.

James Jones — *Blood That Cries Out from the Earth: The Psychology of Religious Terrorism.* New York: Oxford University Press USA, 2008.

Farhad Khosrokhavar — *Inside Jihadism: Understanding Jihadi Movements Worldwide*. Boulder, CO: Paradigm Publishers, 2008.

Jonathan Kitsch — *The Grand Inquisitor's Manual: A History of Terror in the Name of God*. New York: HarperOne, 2008.

Bernard Lewis — *The Crisis of Islam: Holy War and Unholy Terror*. New York: Modern Library, 2003.

Joseph Lumbard, ed. — *Islam, Fundamentalism, and the Betrayal of Tradition: Essays by Western Muslim Scholars*. Bloomington, IN: World Wisdom, 2004.

Irshad Manji — *The Trouble with Islam: A Muslim's Call for Reform in Her Faith*. New York: St. Martin's Press, 2004.

Gabriele Marranci — *Understanding Muslim Identity: Rethinking Fundamentalism*. New York: Palgrave Macmillan, 2009.

Laurent Murawiec — *The Mind of Jihad*. New York: Cambridge University Press, 2008.

John F. Murphy Jr. — *Sword of Islam: Muslim Extremism from the Arab Conquests to the Attack on America*. Amherst, NY: Prometheus Books, 2002.

Omar Nasiri — *Inside the Jihad: My Life with Al-Qaeda*. New York: Perseus Books, 2006.

Princess Palmer — *At the Heart of Terror: Islam, Jihadists, and America's War on Terrorism.* Lanham, MD: Rowman & Littlefield, 2004.

Alison Pargeter — *The New Frontiers of Jihad: Radical Islam in Europe.* Philadelphia: University of Pennsylvania Press, 2008.

Walid Phares — *The War of Ideas: Jihadism Against Democracy.* New York: Palgrave Macmillan, 2008.

Melanie Phillips — *Londonistan.* New York: Encounter Books, 2006.

Daniel Pipes — *Militant Islam Reaches America.* New York: W.W. Norton, 2002.

Ahmed Rashid — *Jihad: The Rise of Militant Islam in Central Asia.* New Haven, CT: Yale University Press, 2002.

Olivier Roy — *The Politics of Chaos in the Middle East.* New York: Columbia University Press, 2008.

Marc Sageman — *Leaderless Jihad: Terror Networks in the Twenty-First Century.* Philadelphia: University of Pennsylvania Press, 2008.

Shamit Saggar — *Pariah Politics: Understanding Western Islamist Extremism and What Should Be Done.* New York: Oxford University Press USA, 2008.

Stephen Schwartz — *The Two Faces of Islam: Saudi Fundamentalism and Its Role in Terrorism*. New York: Anchor Books, 2003.

Zachary Shore — *Breeding Bin Ladens: America, Islam, and the Future of Europe*. Baltimore, MD: Johns Hopkins University Press, 2006.

Robert Spencer — *Stealth Jihad: How Islam Is Subverting America Without Guns Or Bombs*. Washington, DC: Regnery Publishing, 2008.

Devin R. Springer, James L. Regens, and David N. Edger — *Islamic Radicalism and Global Jihad*. Washington, DC: Georgetown University Press, 2009.

Steph Vertigans — *Militant Islam: A Sociology of Characteristics, Causes and Consequences*. New York: Routledge, 2008.

Index